ECONOMIC GROWTH
Unleashing the Potential of Human Flourishing

ECONOMIC GROWTH
Unleashing the Potential of Human Flourishing

Edd S. Noell
Westmont College

Stephen L. S. Smith
Gordon College

Bruce G. Webb
Gordon College

AEI Press
Washington, D.C.

Distributed by arrangement with the Rowman & Littlefield Publishing Group, 4501 Forbes Boulevard, Suite 200, Lanham, MD 20706. To order call toll free 1-800-462-6420 or 1-717-794-3800.

For all other inquiries please contact AEI Press, 1150 17th Street, N.W., Washington, D.C. 20036 or call 1-800-862-5801.

Noell, Edd.
  Economic growth : unleashing the potential of human flourishing / Edd S. Noell, Westmont College, Stephen L. S. Smith, Gordon College, Bruce G. Webb, Gordon College.
    pages cm
  Includes bibliographical references.
  ISBN 978-0-8447-7256-1 (pbk.) -- ISBN 0-8447-7256-9 (pbk.)
  ISBN 978-0-8447-7257-8 (ebook) -- ISBN 0-8447-7257-7 (ebook)
  1. Economic development. 2. Economic development-
  Government policy. 3. Sustainable development. I. Title.
  HD82.N64 2013
  338.9--dc23

CONTENTS

ACKNOWLEDGMENTS

We thank Greg Lane, Karin Agness, and the staff of the American Enterprise Institute's Values & Capitalism project for their encouragement and helpful comments as this book moved from hope to reality. Three anonymous reviewers provided cogent comments on the first draft; we have adopted many of their suggestions, and the book is very much the better as a result. Its remaining faults are entirely our own. Finally, we wish gratefully to acknowledge financial support from a 2011–2012 Mini-Grant in Free Market Economics from the Council of Christian Colleges and Universities.

1

INTRODUCTION: GROWTH IS A MORAL ISSUE

For almost all of the ten thousand years of recorded history, the vast majority of humanity had to eke out a subsistence living in pain and difficulty. Only those with some claim to royalty or privilege enjoyed a chance of a flourishing economic life—though even they were subject to diseases and afflictions now eradicated in our wealthy contemporary world. The deep poverty that was the global norm for most of human history is almost entirely foreign to modern Americans. Living some 260 years after the Industrial Revolution began (in Britain, around 1750), typical twenty-first century citizens have little sense of how unusual, in human historic terms, is the material prosperity that surrounds us. What caused the burst of well-being from which we benefit? Why is so much of the world still poor? Are the rich countries—Europe, Japan, the United States, and a handful of others—so rich that they need no longer worry about material well-being? Can countries become poor again, or stagnate, after getting rich?

Economic growth was the key that transformed societies from dire poverty to prosperity and well-being. It has brought billions of people out of poverty and holds the promise of sustaining even higher levels of human flourishing if it continues. Understanding growth, and answering the important questions posed above, is in part a matter of understanding the economics of growth. But because growth is foundational to material well-being, it is also fundamentally a moral issue. People who care about human well-being, and who care about the poor, should promote growth. Devising policies to promote and sustain growth, in rich and poor countries, is a moral imperative.

This book explores the basic economics of growth alongside of growth's important moral implications. It aims to clarify the moral urgency of thinking clearly about growth. Because economic growth marks a boundary between wealth and human flourishing, on one side, and poverty and degradation, on the other, it is no exaggeration to say that fewer issues are more important. Indeed, as Nobel Prize–winning economist Robert Lucas famously remarked in considering why some economies grow and others do not, "The consequences for human welfare involved in questions like these are simply staggering: once one starts to think about them, it is hard to think about anything else."[1]

Economists use the term "economic growth" to mean a sustained increase in the economy's overall output of goods and services (gross domestic product, or GDP) or a sustained increase in overall output per person, often called a country's "standard of living." For thinking about economic well-being, the latter is preferable. (Growth of total output of, say, 2 percent, leaves the average person worse off if the population is growing at 3 percent.) Because those producing output require payment, a nation's output basically equals its income, so GDP is often called "gross domestic income." When GDP per person rises, average incomes are rising.

Consider what the size of, and growth in, GDP per person tell us about the human condition over time. Estimates of the world's average income in 1000 AD put it at approximately $690 when expressed in dollars comparable in value to US dollars in 2012.[2] What did that income mean, practically, for people living then? Of course, the modern conveniences of global electronic communication, vivid entertainment, and rapid transportation were nonexistent. Homes were dark and cramped; dirt floors and smoky interiors were standard. In a "world lit only by fire" (to use William Manchester's famous book title) light after sundown was precious and hard to come by. Literacy was unusual (who could afford to educate a young person?) and secondary schooling unimaginable (what family could afford to give up an adolescent's work, even if such schooling existed?). But these kinds of deprivations were but the tip of things; the deeper issues were physical. Life was grueling and painful, full of hard labor with nothing but the roughest medical care, all compounded by the slimmest margin of protection against the weather.

Over the next eight centuries, to 1820, the world's average annual growth rate in income per person was about 0.05 percent—a vanishingly small number. In what is now Western Europe it averaged almost three times that rate—0.13 percent per year through 1500, then 0.15 percent per year through 1820—but was still very low. At these growth rates, progress in material well-being was imperceptible from decade to decade. By 1500, the power of compounding had raised average product per person to $890 in the world as a whole and $1,200 in Europe (which went from being one of the poorest regions of the world to the richest). By 1820, when the Industrial Revolution had finally taken hold in most of Europe and the Napoleonic Wars were over, average incomes were about $1,050 in the world as a whole and $1,950 in Europe.

Despite this measurable progress from 1000 AD, the 1820 income levels were appallingly low. We catch a glimpse of exactly how low, and of the physical and emotional pain of everyday life, in the life expectancies of that era. In Western Europe, life expectancy was just 36 years, and it was a tragically low 24 years in the rest of the world. These low life expectancies were caused in part by dreadful infant mortality rates (IMRs, which measure infant deaths per 1,000 live births). England's IMR was shockingly high at 144, while France's was around 180 and Japan's was in the mid-200s. Contrast those measures with contemporary IMRs of 5, 3, and 2 for the UK, France, and Japan, respectively, and life expectancies in the high 70s and low 80s.[3]

From the early 1800s onward, the rate of economic growth accelerated dramatically in some parts of the world, notably Europe, the United States and Canada, and Japan. Across the whole sweep of the 1800s and 1900s, annual income growth per person averaged more than 1.5 percent in Europe and more than 1.7 percent in the United States. (Annual growth rates often exceeded 2 percent but were offset by wars and other disruptions.) Expressed in contemporary values, the average income in the United States went from approximately $1,980 in 1820 to $43,200 in 2000. These stupendous increases in incomes drove the dramatic improvements in physical well-being that we modern citizens take for granted.

Until the 1600s, the concept of economic growth was not really recognized. For those seeking to steer a nation's economic performance, the goal was generally to enhance the nation's power or wealth, and wealth was largely conceived in terms of the stock of precious metals in the king's treasury. Only in the past few centuries has economic growth been carefully discussed and set out as a major

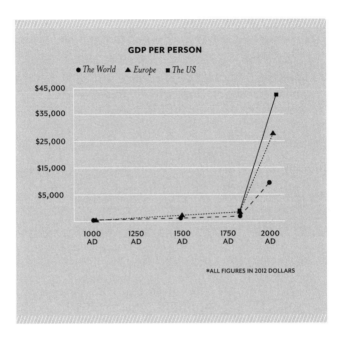

GDP PER PERSON

● *The World*   ▲ *Europe*   ■ *The US*

*ALL FIGURES IN 2012 DOLLARS

macroeconomic policy goal. Slowly, over the course of the 1800s and early 1900s, economic growth came to be valued for its huge positive effects in raising human welfare (and national power).

This change is evident in modern public debate about the future of America's economic performance. In some quarters, concerns are expressed about our long-run ability to sustain improvements in economic well-being. Economic

TABLE 1. ECONOMIC GROWTH IN THE UNITED STATES, 1960–2009

DECADE	AVERAGE ANNUAL GROWTH RATE (%)
1960–1969	3.1
1970–1979	2.2
1980–1989	2.1
1990–1999	1.9
2000–2009	0.7

Source: Authors' calculations based on GDP data from Bureau of Economic Analysis, www.bea.gov/national/index.htm#gdp, and population data from Bureau of the Census, www.census.gov. Note: The rates are based on per capita real income calculated in 2005 dollars.

growth in the United States has indeed slowed appreciably in the last half century. The average annual rate of increase in real income per person has fallen steadily in each of the last five decades, from 3.1 percent in the 1960s to 0.7 percent in the first decade of the 2000s (see table 1). Some of this slowdown is due to the fact that countries on the cutting edge of technology, like the United States, do not grow as rapidly as other countries (a trend discussed in later chapters). Nonetheless, the trend is real, and it makes a difference. At a growth rate of 2.5 percent per person per year, real income doubles in about 29 years; at 1 percent, doubling takes more than 72 years. Furthermore, many politicians and analysts worry about the slow, uneven recovery from the 2008 financial crisis, which has been characterized by stubbornly high unemployment and stagnant household incomes—a concern more about immediate growth than long-term growth.

At the same time, critics of economic growth have gained ground in recent years. They have argued that economic growth is responsible for environmental damage, places humankind on an unsustainable trajectory, and fosters greater income inequality. Some have offered strongly voiced moral objections to economic growth—for instance, that insisting upon economic growth is selfish, materialistic, and an invitation to rampant consumerism.

This book argues that economic growth generates and is necessary for broad improvements in humanity's material well-being. These improvements go far beyond mere access to modern conveniences, such as travel, entertainment, and communication (though these valuable items are themselves both fruits and means of growth). Growth undergirds the social wealth that provides fundamental improvements in health, education, and housing. By improving national finances, growth makes such fundamental improvements sustainable. These benefits of growth are enjoyed in developing economies—dramatic poverty reductions have occurred over the past four decades in developing countries with sustained high rates of economic growth—as well as in the United States and other rich countries.

Furthermore, growth remains essential for long-term human flourishing, understood in moral terms. Because growth helps the poor, its effects on inequality (often overstated in any case) should not hinder pursuing growth. Because growth is good for the environment, the gains it brings to the poor and to the rich should not be traded away in pursuit of environmental sustainability. Because growth and the market institutions that sustain it have substantial moral benefits, market systems should not be sacrificed in the name of preserving morality, despite markets' shortcomings. Because growth helps avoid fiscal and debt crises in both rich and poor countries, it can ease problems (such as paying for Social Security and other retirement programs) that would otherwise pit young against old in painful intergenerational conflict. Whether the focus is on equality, the environment, markets, or demographic pressures, actual growth experiences of the past century support the judgment that growth is good for human flourishing.

Though the record of growth's benefits is compelling, economic analysis alone cannot sustain a social consensus for growth. Economic approaches cannot inspire the moral imagination. Societies must be convinced of growth's moral legitimacy, and of the merits of the market-oriented systems in which growth blooms, if a consensus for growth is to develop. Because the authors of this book all teach at Christian colleges, we are interested in how growth relates to Christian moral norms in particular as well as to moral questions more generally, and we address both in the course of the book. While economic growth has been controversial among Christian thinkers, we will make the case for its moral legitimacy and its consistency with Christian norms such as creativity and stewardship. The moral issues we consider have near-universal resonance, so our exploration of growth's moral underpinnings is designed to help Christians and non-Christians alike to think clearly about growth.

The book lays out the economic and moral case for growth as follows. Chapter 2 considers the sources of growth in technological innovations, capital and labor accumulation, and, especially, institutions and policies. Chapter 3 reviews the empirical evidence about growth (which critics routinely ignore or misjudge). It examines how economic research, particularly as it focuses on the links between growth and improved income inequality, buttresses the case for growth. Chapters 4 and 5 consider the economic and moral objections to economic growth: the impacts of growth on the environment (including environmental damage and the question of sustainability) and growth's effects on character and the human community. Chapter 6 examines the two-way relation between growth and government budgets and shows that growth helps countries contend with demographic pressures, debt, and inflation. Chapter 7 assesses the importance to economic growth of market institutions and policy choices, including legal property protection, enforcement of contracts, and encouragement of technological innovation. Finally, Chapter 8 provides a brief discussion of growth's fragility and summarizes the case that growth is essential for human flourishing.

2

SOURCES OF GROWTH

Knowing the sources of economic growth is essential for understanding it. But before looking at these sources, this chapter explores why economists prefer to use GDP per person as the basic yardstick to measure growth, economic well-being, and the "standard of living." This approach sheds light on the nature of growth and its link to human flourishing.

GDP per person is not an ideal measure of the standard of living. Its shortcomings are well known. It counts only goods and services produced for sale, leaving out valuable goods and services produced by households for their own use (such as food a family grows for itself, and child care provided by family members), or produced for barter. Basing growth analysis on GDP per person can also mask income-distribution problems, because increases in the average do not necessarily mean that everyone's income is rising. Another potentially serious problem is that GDP, which basically measures an annual flow of income, does not reflect trends in national assets. For instance, if an environmentally valuable old-growth forest is harvested, measured GDP will rise—but the country may be less wealthy in the sense of having lost a valuable asset (just as a family would be less wealthy if it were to raise money by selling the household silver). The best solution to this problem is to keep track of national assets directly, in a separate account, just as firms keep separate income and asset accounts.

Despite all these problems, per capita GDP is the best single yardstick available for measuring economic growth. Its great strength is that it captures the fundamental availability of goods and services, and of income to spend on goods and services. A country with a GDP of $10,000 per person has fundamentally more ability to provide goods and services to its residents than one with a GDP of $2,000 per person. All else equal, people living in the first country will have more access to housing, health care, education, and all the opportunities that resources provide. A country growing at 3 percent per person per year will, over time, have more goods and services available than one growing at 1 percent per person per year. That is not to say that poorer countries cannot do some basic things; some poor countries do better than others at providing education, for instance. But across the board, a bigger GDP means that a country can do more to provide the whole range of goods and services that contribute to human well-being.

The evidence of this is vivid. GDP per capita is very strongly correlated with virtually every important indicator of human development. Female and male literacy? Longevity? Reductions in mortality rates for children under five? Poverty reduction? Environmental regulation? Higher education? Name your measure, and GDP per capita and growth in GDP per capita are strong predictors of progress in it. For instance, the correlation between GDP per capita and reductions in the under-five mortality rate is 0.87, an eye-poppingly large and statistically significant association.[4] The historical and likely future connections between economic growth and health more broadly have been reinforced by research by Robert Fogel, a Nobel economics laureate. Fogel finds that if economic growth continues in the twenty-first century, it will allow us to live longer and devote a much smaller fraction of our lives to paid work, raising lifetime leisure hours.[5]

GDP per capita also helps clarify a significant element of income inequality issues. Many countries struggle with income distribution problems, and populist, redistributive policies are a constant temptation for governments looking for quick fixes. Nigeria, for instance, has a rich upper class that numbers in the millions. Could not the plight of Nigeria's poor be addressed with radical income-redistribution policies rather than with economic growth? Why should the government not promise free education or free health care for everyone, immediately, and simply grab the necessary resources from the rich? Nigeria's 2009 per capita income of

$1,980 shows us the problem with this approach.[6] Complete equality in Nigeria would leave everyone extremely poor. It would barely make a dent in the poverty of Nigeria's less affluent citizens. For raising material well-being, there is no alternative to growth. Redistribution alone will never be sufficient for sustained, shared improvement in living standards.

SPECIALIZATION, TRADE, AND ECONOMIC GROWTH

Adam Smith, often called the father of economics, was the first to write a comprehensive account of the meaning and possibility of economic growth. In his most famous work, *An Inquiry into the Nature and Causes of the Wealth of Nations* (1776), Smith argued that it was possible for all nations to increase their wealth by adopting policies that promote specialization and the division of labor.

The prevailing view that Smith criticized was mercantilism, which held that wealth consisted of the stock of precious metals in a country. To increase wealth of this sort, a nation needed to sell more goods to other countries than it purchased from them, thus accumulating more precious metals ("specie" or money in the form, literally, of gold and silver). Since these metals were in relatively fixed supply, the only way one country could get more was at the expense of another country. One country's gain was equivalent to another country's loss. The pursuit of wealth was thus a zero-sum game, which meant that other countries were viewed as economic rivals.

Smith opposed the mercantilists on two counts. First, he rejected their narrow view of wealth. Smith argued that a nation's wealth not only consisted of precious metals but also included its entire stock of valuable goods, from factories to houses to ploughs to shoes—anything produced to satisfy some need or want. Second, he maintained that the stock of wealth (rightly understood) could be increased by stepping up the production of valuable goods, and that this increased production could be achieved by more efficient allocation of labor—that is, by specialization and division of labor. In Smith's words,

> The greatest improvements in the productive powers of labour, and the greater part of the skill, dexterity, and judgment with which it is any where directed, or applied, seem to have been the effects of the division of labour.[7]

Smith gave the example of pin making, which seems simple but could be broken down into several distinct operations. When each worker focused on one distinct task, all workers became more productive, and many more pins could be produced than if each worker had to learn, perform, and switch among several tasks. Smith highlighted the gains from exchange that result when individuals or firms specialize in producing different products. We take these gains for granted today, without realizing how profound are the benefits of being able to specialize in one job (say, auto mechanic) and exchanging for (that is, buying) virtually everything else that we need without having to make it ourselves.

Smith extended his argument to include specialization by countries:

> What is prudence in the conduct of every private family can scarce be folly in that of a great kingdom. If a foreign country can supply us with a commodity cheaper than we ourselves can make it, better buy it of them with some part of the produce of our own industry, employed in a way in which we have some advantage.[8]

According to this view, nations can all benefit by trade. They need not be economic rivals. Since Smith's time, economists have learned a great deal more about the sources of each country's "natural advantages," which give rise to international trade. But modern studies support Smith's main conclusion: countries that engage in trade and participate in the global economy grow faster than countries that do not.[9]

SAVING, INVESTMENT, TECHNOLOGY, AND ECONOMIC GROWTH

Modern analysis of economic growth started in the 1950s with the economist Robert Solow, who developed what came to be called the "Solow model" of economic growth. The Solow model and its extensions are based on the idea that the main drivers of economic growth are saving and investment in physical and human capital. A country's domestic saving is the total of personal (household) saving, business saving (profits not paid in taxes or to owners/stockholders), and government saving (equal to the government's budget surplus—tax revenues minus government outlays). In reality, many governments run budget deficits rather than surpluses; in those cases, government saving is negative. As discussed in chapter 6, deficits can slow the rate of economic growth.

A country with a high domestic savings rate and/or large inflows of foreign savings provides, through financial markets, more funds for businesses to borrow to finance investment in physical capital (machines, buildings, computers, etc.). Giving workers more physical capital makes them more productive. If countries that start with small amounts of physical capital per worker increase savings and efficiently invest in physical capital, they can grow rapidly. For rich countries with relatively large amounts of capital per worker, further increases in capital are likely to run into the problem of diminishing returns—that is, increases in capital per worker lead to smaller and smaller increases in worker productivity. Growth based solely on physical capital accumulation inevitably runs out of steam. The fact that countries with large amounts of capital per worker can still experience growth suggests that we must look to a second form of capital, and to technological change, as other important components of growth.

Economists call that other type of capital "human capital." Human capital consists of the knowledge and skills possessed by workers. Just as for physical capital, to build up the stock of human capital requires investment. Education costs money, and it can be expensive for workers (and society) to forgo years of paid employment in order to acquire an education. (College students are keenly aware of this opportunity cost of human capital acquisition!) Increases in the quality and quantity of education, and in formalized or informal on-the-job training, all build human capital. Unlike physical capital, human capital is not used up in the process of producing goods and services, and it benefits the individual and society in ways over and above its effect on productivity. Investment in human capital is similar to investment in physical capital in that it boosts the productivity of labor—and in that there are diminishing returns to this productivity boost. For instance, on average in the United States, people with college degrees earn 65 percent more than people with only high school diplomas; but people with master's degrees earn only 20 percent more than college graduates' earnings.[10]

Through a process known as growth accounting, economists quickly realized that the Solow model's emphasis on saving and investment in physical and human capital left a large part of economic growth unexplained. Increases in physical and human capital explain only a small portion of observed growth. The substantial unexplained portion is due to technological change that increases the productivity of both types of capital. Studies over the past sixty years have generally found that approximately half of all economic growth can be attributed to acquisition of more capital, labor, and natural resources, and about half can be attributed to technological change.[11] What brings about technological change? The Solow model left this question unanswered.

RECENT THEORIES OF ECONOMIC GROWTH

To explain technological change, economists have focused recently on the importance of new ideas as sources of what is called "cutting-edge" growth. Unlike physical and human capital, ideas can be shared by many producers at the same time; making the ideas available to one producer does not diminish the amount available to others. Ideas that promote economic growth can range from the development of new products (e.g., smart phones), to new production methods (e.g., restructuring the workplace), to the development of new technologies (e.g., nanotechnologies).

Some technological innovations are modest and incremental. Others have substantial effects that can raise productivity in—even transform—many industries. These latter technologies are called general purpose technologies (GPTs). A good example is electricity. The slow diffusion and adoption of electric power during the late 1800s and early 1900s literally transformed the industrial landscape the world over—firms no longer needed to be located near water, or rely on steam engines, for power. It also transformed household life, though these effects took longer to play out. A current example of a GPT is the Internet, whose long-term effects on productivity will be substantial but are not yet fully realized. Incremental technological change and GPTs lead to economic growth because new products and new productive techniques drive economic reorganization and transformation, so that the economy yields greater output from any given set of physical capital, natural inputs, and labor.

Cutting-edge growth is relevant for countries that have already invested heavily in physical and human capital and thus face the problem of diminishing returns. Such countries may be able to sustain annual per capita income growth rates of 2 to 4 percent if incremental technological change and development of GPTs continue, stimulated by research and development spending and institutions friendly to technological change and diffusion. Barring demographic crises, serious economic policy mistakes, or other calamities, such growth should be able to continue indefinitely. Of course, because of the power of compound growth rates over time, even the present-day rich countries should consider what policies will keep them toward the high end of the feasible growth rate range. Over the course of twenty years, for instance, growth at 3.5 percent per person per year will double income, while 2.0 percent per person per year raises income only by about 50 percent.

Why is India growing so much faster than the United States and other rich countries? Why has China had three decades of per capita income growth averaging over 8 percent per year—a blistering pace matched only by Korea and Japan in their growth bursts of the late 1900s? To answer these questions, it is helpful to make a distinction between cutting-edge growth and "catch-up" growth.[12] Unlike cutting-edge growth, which takes place in rich and developed countries, catch-up growth can occur in poor countries where there is a relatively small capital stock, where investment in physical and human capital has a big payoff, and where established technologies can be adopted and copied. (A country with a relatively large capital stock, such as the United States, has already invested in many of the available high-return projects and so must look elsewhere for continued growth.) With the right policy choices, poor countries can indeed grow much faster than the present-day rich countries (and faster than the latter grew, historically). This is a promising feature of growth. It means that the present wide disparities in incomes around the world need not be permanent, and can be addressed over decades, not centuries.

THE CRUCIAL ROLE OF INSTITUTIONS

But there is more to the story of economic growth than capital accumulation and technological change. Why do accumulation and technological progress occur? What makes these processes rapid at times and slow at others? The answers lie in countries' different economic institutions and policies, which themselves are embedded in and arise from culture, geography, and history. Economists have understood for many years that institutions play a crucial role in shaping economic growth. But only in recent decades have economists looked closely at questions of institutions and institutional development.[13]

Social and political institutions shape human interaction by structuring incentives and constraints; they establish the rules of the game of economic exchange and help determine property rights, technological innovation, and regulation of economic activity. Economists generally agree that market-oriented economic institutions, such as secure property rights and the rule of law, are needed to encourage investment in physical and human capital. Other kinds of institutions are less effective at that task or, in fact, actively impede it.

What happened in Britain during and following the first Industrial Revolution is an outstanding example of the key role played by economic institutions in encouraging sustained economic growth. While economic institutions in Western Europe from the 1500s onward developed in ways that encouraged growth, the British Industrial Revolution, which spanned the period 1750–1850, represented the flowering of those institutions. Between the 1500s and the 1700s, Britain developed a strong, pliable structure of property rights; Douglass North has argued that the English Parliament's implementation of laws based on the principle of noninterference with private property constituted market-oriented reforms.[14] According to Daron Acemoglu and James Robinson, these laws protecting private property created significantly greater incentive to "invest in physical or human capital or adopt more efficient technologies" than had existed in their absence.[15]

Another dynamic that contributed to Britain's remarkable economic performance as the first industrial nation was a market-friendly culture that encouraged positive attitudes toward exchange, and market activity, in general. The economic historian Joel Mokyr observes that

> what mattered for economic performance was a level of confidence that made it possible to transact with non-kin, and increasingly with people who were almost strangers. Market activity, and especially transactions at arm's length, increased throughout the period of the Industrial Revolution at ever accelerating rates. This happened, oddly enough, in an age during which the costs of legal action went up, its availability and efficiency were declining, and as a result fewer and fewer people took recourse to the law.[16]

In short, in that time and place there was broad cultural support for the legitimacy of market transactions and for norms that promoted the trustworthiness of market participants. Generalized social trust acted as a kind of social capital that helped to promote investment and entrepreneurship. Cultural support for growth and for the market remains a crucial element of continued growth in rich and poor countries alike.

What does our survey of the sources and nature of growth imply for government policies? Top-down, command-and-control economic policies (favored by socialist nations and occasionally adopted by other authoritarian regimes) may work for a time. Postindependence India, for example, experienced some growth when its government mimicked the Soviet Union and used central planning to pour resources into steel and capital goods industries.

> "Generalized social trust acted as a kind of social capital that helped to promote investment and entrepreneurship. Cultural support for growth and for the market remains a crucial element of continued growth in rich and poor countries alike."

Such policies are effective initially—especially when well-established technologies are adopted from abroad and a regime is interested only in catch-up growth. But they inevitably run aground on the punishingly high costs of subsidizing selected favored industries (which penalizes all other industries), and on the extraordinary inefficiencies inherent in centralized economic decision making.

Governments seeking to unlock long-term growth should eschew command-and-control policies. Instead, they should craft economic institutions that reward all types of investment in physical and human capital, and that help markets function securely and inexpensively. For instance, an impartial judicial system that defines and enforces clear property rights gives firms and individuals the right incentives for work and investment; they know the courts will adjudicate property claims and contract disputes fairly, and uphold the rule of law. Other key institutions include a stable, relatively corruption-free government, one that is able to provide for national defense and other public goods; a market system for the production and distribution of most goods and services, to provide monetary incentives for efficient allocation of resources and creation of jobs and incomes without need of government control or subsidy; and a financial system, modestly regulated for safety and paired with a sound currency, to encourage savings and to channel those savings into loans for large and small firms.

It is instructive to consider why some countries (such as Haiti and the Central African Republic) have not achieved even modest levels of growth since the mid-1990s. These countries' populations constitute what economist Paul Collier has called the "bottom billion."[17] In the 1990s, when growth was strong in most of the world, incomes in these countries fell by 5 percent. According to Collier, these countries face one or more "traps" that prevent them from attaining growth levels that many other developing countries have recently achieved. One is the natural resources trap: the existence of extraordinary profits from natural resources such as oil tempts ruling elites to grab the profits and use them to keep themselves in power, while the development of the natural resource industry drains investments from the rest of the economy. Another is the conflict trap, in which countries are either engaged in civil war or just emerging from it. Destruction of infrastructure stops growth in its tracks and breeds poverty and resentment, setting the stage for repeated civil war. Strikingly, these traps hinge on the absence of strong market-oriented institutions and stable governance. The rule of law is absent. Economic life is understood as a zero-sum, winner-take-all game in which the state serves the interests of the current power-holder; neither the wider national interest nor wealth creation is a priority. Civil society institutions and healthy state institutions are missing.

IN SUM

Though not a perfect measure of well-being, income per capita measures the availability of goods and services in a society and therefore is highly positively correlated with all kinds of human welfare improvements, including health, longevity, education, and pollution control. Poverty reduction cannot be achieved simply through redistribution, particularly in poor countries; growth and structural transformation are necessary to raise material standards of living and human well-being to levels that allow human flourishing. The immediate sources of growth are physical and human capital accumulation and technological change. But over the long run, in countries enjoying cutting-edge growth, these sources are themselves rooted in social institutions, government policies, and cultural norms that are friendly to markets and that protect property rights. Institutions and policies are important enough that we revisit them in greater detail in chapter 7.

3

**GROWTH, POVERTY,
AND INEQUALITY**

How does growth affect poverty and income distribution over the long run? There have been persistent worries about this question among critics of growth. Critics may point to the example of the United States, which has since 1980 experienced a gradual widening of its income distribution; current US college students' only experience with a growing economy has been one in which income gaps keep increasing. Other countries also provide cautionary evidence. Saudi Arabia is nominally rich but has extremes of wealth and poverty. New oil wealth in Equatorial Guinea since the early 1990s has fueled enormous economic growth, very little of which has helped its poor, who remain stuck in absolute poverty. Is a wide gap between rich and poor a necessary feature of growth in the long run?

It is helpful to approach this question at two levels. We look first at growth's effects within individual countries and then consider the world as a whole.

THE EFFECT OF GROWTH WITHIN NATIONS

Detailed household surveys reveal a consistent picture: over the past fifty years and across many nations, rich and poor, there is a strong positive relationship between a nation's overall per capita income and the per capita income of its poor. In percentage terms, the relationship is virtually one for one: a 10 percent increase in a nation's (overall) average income is associated with about a 10 percent increase in the average income of its poor.[18] This means that growth has little impact on the share of national income received by the poor—and raises the poor out of absolute poverty because their income rises along with everyone else's.

There is some variation in this pattern. While in most countries the share of national income earned by the poorest 20 percent of households (the poorest quintile) rises or stays the same as growth occurs, in others the lowest quintile's share of national income falls. Note that even in these latter cases the absolute income earned by the poor can rise. For instance, if a country's income doubles but the poor go from earning 6 percent of national income to 5 percent, in absolute dollar terms the poor on average have much higher incomes than before—they have a slightly smaller share of a much larger pie. This situation explains the overwhelming evidence that in rich and poor countries alike economic growth raises absolute income for all income groups and thus reduces the extent of absolute poverty.

This situation obtains, for instance, in the United States. The share of all US income earned by the lowest quintile has fallen since the 1970s—hence the measured increase in US inequality.[19] But the real command over resources of the poorest quintile has grown a lot. Including earned compensation (such as employer-paid health care and other benefits) and government transfer payments such as welfare, and adjusting for household size, the lowest quintile had 26 percent more real income in 2007 than in 1979. Middle-income households also saw substantial gains—37 percent—notwithstanding common perceptions that middle-class incomes have stagnated in recent years.[20]

There is particularly strong evidence that growth-driven poverty reduction has occurred in some of the poorest parts of the world in the past three or four decades. Consider a baseline "$1.25 per day" poverty measure, the proportion of a country's population who consume at this level or below. World Bank figures show that on this basis, China's poverty rate fell from 84 percent in 1981 to 13 percent in 2008,[21] a period that exactly coincides with that nation's growth-unleashing market-oriented reforms. Likewise, sub-Saharan Africa's poverty rate was as high as 59 percent in the 1990s, but fell to 48 percent in 2008, during that continent's growth resurgence. India's poverty rate fell from 66 percent in 1978 to 42 percent in 2005, while real GDP grew 5.4 percent per year on average over that period (and grew 6.3 percent per year in the reform era after 1991). Interestingly, while China's and India's absolute poverty rates have both fallen, their income distributions have moved differently: the share of income earned by China's poorest quintile fell from more than 10 percent in the early 1980s to around 7 percent in the early 2000s, while the share earned by India's lowest quintile held steady at around 9 percent in the same period.[22]

Why does economic growth almost always raise the real incomes of the poor? Growth sets changes in motion that invariably increase opportunities for all groups in society. The explosion of call-center services in India, for instance, sharply increased demand for literate English speakers, who rank as relatively high- and medium-skilled workers in the Indian economy. But this demand triggered changes that also increased demand for low-skilled labor in construction, food service, and myriad other fields. For poor countries integrated in world trade, increases in demand for labor sparked by trade tend to raise demand for low-skilled labor, because poor countries' comparative-advantage products tend (initially) to be labor-intensive goods and services. This demand for low-skilled labor helps the poor directly. Furthermore, as national income rises, any extra government spending on social services for the poor—health and education spending, in particular—boosts their earnings potential. As Collier has observed, "overwhelmingly, the problem of the bottom billion has not been that they have had the wrong type of growth, it is that they have not had any growth."[23] For all practical purposes, income growth in a poor nation as a whole results in poverty reduction in that country.

Then what accounts for the fact that as growth occurs, some countries' income distributions become more equal, while others become less equal? Nations' own domestic policy choices have a big impact on the actual income-distribution and poverty-reducing consequences of their growth. For instance, India's continued restrictions on its manufacturing sector have blunted the increase in demand for low-skilled labor arising from its recent economic growth. Other countries have wasted lots of money on unwise investments in high-tech industries or have neglected investments in education and health care for the poor. Policies that restrain trade in order to protect an economy from foreign competition have proven particularly damaging for the poor. They may promote growth for a season—they were popular in the 1960s and 1970s before their full growth-sapping costs became undeniable—but by putting a premium on high-skilled labor and making all kinds of consumer goods more expensive, they hurt the poor. The policy lessons here are clear: growth helps the poor most when governments avoid policies that raise demand for high-skilled labor at the expense of low-skilled labor, when governments fund generous investments in basic education and health, and when governments pursue policies of broad global economic engagement rather than economic disengagement. In the US case, a big driver of recent worsening in the income distribution has not been growth per se but technological change that has reduced demand for low-skilled workers while raising demand for high-skilled workers, a phenomenon experienced across most rich countries. Another contributing factor has been changes in family structures, particularly increased divorce rates, which have increased the number of single-income families.

THE EFFECT OF GROWTH ACROSS NATIONS

Compound growth is powerful and asserts itself inexorably over time. Since the 1970s, many large-population developing countries such as China, India, Indonesia, and Vietnam have grown at faster rates than rich countries; this basic fact means that for the world as a whole, incomes are converging. When growth rates in poor countries are higher than growth rates in rich countries, gaps between nations' average incomes recede. The early twenty-first century is an era of income growth and global convergence, not divergence; the global income distribution has become more equal since the mid-1970s.

This is one of the least understood, but nonetheless most striking, features of the present globalization era. For the first time in close to five hundred years, the global income distribution is improving. Yet many commentators persist in the view that the global income distribution is worsening, and that divides in the global economy are sharper now than ever.

Several features of growth contribute to this misperception. The very poorest countries of the world have experienced little growth in the past fifty or sixty years, so comparisons between them and the rest of the world show increased absolute divergences. But because only a small portion of the world's people live in these extremely poor countries, such as Haiti, the growing absolute gap between the very richest and poorest countries does not reveal much about overall global income distribution.

A more subtle cause of the misperception that global income inequality is rising comes from the widespread correct, but misunderstood, observation that in China and elsewhere income distributions have worsened. China's enormous population means that its income growth has noticeably pushed up average income in the world as a whole and makes world incomes more equal. That China's internal income distribution is becoming less equal pulls the global income distribution the other way, toward more inequality; but this effect is small compared to the first effect, which has been massive. Overall, the global income distribution has become more equal because of China's growth and that of other developing countries with large populations.[24]

More good news comes from the global distribution of the economic goods that are highly correlated with income, mentioned earlier. Global inequality in life expectancy, educational attainment, health, and infant mortality is falling. Life expectancy, for instance, has risen more rapidly in poor countries than in rich countries over the past few decades, so the global distribution of life expectancy is now more equal. Evidence from the World Bank is definitive on this point, and it is a major feature of the actual convergence, as opposed to the alleged divergence, of the globalization era. Convergence in this and other important dimensions of human well-being is due in part to aid—particularly in countries where growth has been weak or nonexistent—but is in larger part the direct result of fifty or more years of economic growth in poor regions.[25]

IN SUM

The evidence is clear that economic growth contributes fundamentally to poverty reduction. Hence, there are economic and moral reasons to favor growth; its poverty-reducing potential must be taken seriously by anyone concerned about the poor. Growth should not be shunned because of fears of what it might do to income distribution, within countries or globally. Too much is at stake for the poor. Actual growth experience since the 1970s has seen declines in global income inequality, along with declines in global inequality in education, health, and life expectancy.

4

OBJECTIONS TO GROWTH: ENVIRONMENT AND SUSTAINABILITY

Problems with growth can seem obvious. Few are unmoved at the sight of industrial scrap fouling a beach. Few would argue that life is just a game to be won by accumulating the most goods. Basic moral instincts shared across cultures and religions make many observers wonder if perpetual growth really is intrinsically desirable. Might it destroy the environment? Might it encourage pursuit of material wealth as the highest good?

In a Christian worldview, care for creation is part of mankind's charge from God—part of having dominion (properly understood) and exercising stewardship over the earth. Christian teaching speaks clearly against looking for meaning in material acquisitions, a perspective widely shared across many belief systems. So it is possible to see a moral, religious, and specifically Christian basis for two of the most longstanding and popular critiques of growth. The first is that, in its essence, growth harms the environment and is not sustainable. The second is that its long-term consequences are harmful to human community and well-being. We consider each critique in turn: we treat the environment in this chapter and community in the following chapter.

The Industrial Revolution was dirty. By the 1800s, cities in Britain were covered in soot. China's cities today are the same. Surely racing to modernize and grow causes pollution and environmental degradation.

Surprisingly, the relationship between economic growth and the environment is more complex and subtle than the simplistic hypothesis above suggests. Disputes about how economic growth affects the environment fall broadly into two categories. First, there are disagreements about the extent and trajectory of the ongoing environmental harm caused by growth. Second, there are disputes about the potential for a severe global environmental catastrophe—the possibility that growth might literally exhaust nonrenewable resources such as oil and natural gas, or cause global environmental catastrophes such as global warming–induced rises in sea levels, or mass starvation due to overpopulation. While the two are obviously related, it is helpful to distinguish them.

ENVIRONMENTAL HARM

Growth, particularly rapid initial growth, has caused instances of severe environmental degradation. Yet, surprisingly, the evidence is that over time income growth is compatible with, and may be essential for, environmental protection. In the United States and other nations in the Organisation for Economic Co-operation and Development, by almost any measure the environment is dramatically cleaner now than it was 50 years ago,[26] so it clearly is possible to have simultaneous growth and environmental improvement. Appropriate, democratically arrived at environmental regulation plus the predictable market forces that emerge in the course of economic growth have worked this wonder. Conversely, poverty and authoritarian economic systems—not growth in and of itself—may pose the biggest threats to environmental harm.

Consider a poor country that has yet to experience sustained economic growth. It will likely be neither clean nor green: poverty is a key cause of environmental degradation. Rural dwellers in this country may practice slash and burn agriculture, which causes substantial problems at anything beyond the smallest scale. City dwellers probably do not have septic or sewer systems, so major rivers are clogged with human waste and discharge from small, old-technology factories that have no emissions controls. Farmers and urbanites alike burn coal and dung for heat and cooking, so the air is thick with sooty particles. For such a country, the initial stages of economic growth provide income that can be used almost immediately to improve some aspects of the environment. Once poor societies start to grow, they tend to spend freely on sewage and septic systems, on more expensive fuels such as natural gas that are cleaner than coal, and on many other basic environmental improvements. Thus some kinds of pollution begin to fall as soon as economic growth gets underway.

But some kinds of pollution rise. New factories may be cleaner than older ones, but as industrial output, agricultural output, and urbanization surge, pollution from new sources rises. Internal combustion engines, power plants, and effluent from new manufacturing contribute to an overall rise in pollution. Amazingly to Western sensibilities, surveys show that citizens in poor countries often tolerate this degradation as a necessary cost of growth. They value the rapid rise in income more than they object to the environmental damage that accompanies it.

Over time, at higher levels of income, attitudes change. Environmental protection becomes a priority. It is hard to predict exactly when this change will happen. It is related to attitudes about the environment, and to education and political institutions as well. There is now more awareness of environmental problems in poor countries than there was in prior generations, just as in the West. There thus emerges what researchers call the "environmental Kuznets curve" (EKC)—an inverted-U relation between pollution and income growth. Pollution rises as income rises from low levels, but then falls when a threshold income level is reached.

The existence of the EKC is well documented.[27] Estimates suggest that the turning point in incomes is around $5,000 to $8,000 per person per year in constant purchasing power dollars, a broad range that is affected by all the factors described above. As technologies improve and feature fewer emissions, the level of the EKC may be drifting downward. In the early twenty-first century, countries in their initial growth phases appear to pollute less than

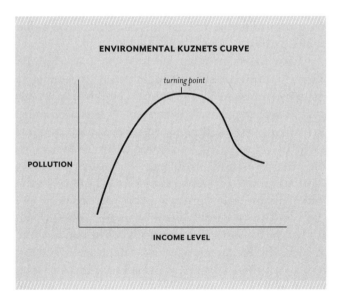

ENVIRONMENTAL KUZNETS CURVE

turning point

POLLUTION

INCOME LEVEL

similar countries did four decades ago when they were at similar stages of growth, and less than the now-developed countries did still earlier. For instance, because of what is now known about the grave risks of PCBs (polychlorinated biphenyls) in the environment, China banned their production in the 1980s, far earlier in its development process than did the United States (1979). China's present boom in auto demand is being filled by cars that are far cleaner than the Fords of the first mass automobile market in the United States. All this bodes well for the environment and for the long-term coexistence of growth and environmental care and protection.

Many kinds of environmental problems are best understood, in economic terms, as "negative externalities" arising from economic activity. That is, they are the consequences of decisions or actions—by firms, households, or governments—that harm those who had no say in the action or decision. A steel firm, for example, might emit polluted water into a river without regard for downstream users. Negative externalities can be evaluated and corrected using several well-understood kinds of policies. Taxing emissions at a rate equal to the emissions' marginal cost to society results in an efficient reduction of the negative externality—a reduction to the socially optimal point where further reductions cost more than the extra benefit they would bring to society. Other kinds of regulation, such as pollution standards (the typical regulatory approach in the United States—for instance, setting maximum allowable "parts per million"), are costlier but also work. Finally, sometimes simply defining and enforcing property rights can clear up a pollution problem. The cute robot WALL-E, in Disney's film of the same name, would not have had any trash to pick up if property rights against dumping had been defined and enforced on his planet!

Some other environmental problems are "common-pool resource" problems, situations where the multiple users of a renewable natural resource do not have clearly defined property rights in it. This gives individual users an incentive to overuse the resource lest others use it up first. For example, fishing boats from multiple nations ply the eastern Pacific, and each boat has an incentive to overfish because if it does not, others will. Another example of a common-pool resource is the North China aquifer, which extends under many provinces. Farmers, households, cities, towns, and factories all tap into it without charge, using the water faster than it can be replenished. Carbon emissions in the atmosphere that cause global warming are yet another kind of common-pool resource problem (considered later in this section). The stakes are high in common-pool resource problems, because the resource really can be destroyed; for example, cod have virtually disappeared from parts of the western Atlantic due to overfishing, as governments' fishing bans came too late to allow stocks to regenerate.

Policy solutions for common-pool resource problems exist but can be hard to implement. Within a nation, well-defined, enforceable property rights give owners incentives to protect resources. Internationally, treaties can govern rates of use or harvesting. Such agreements get progressively harder to negotiate and enforce, however, as more firms, provinces, and nations are involved—the free rider problem complicates things. Yet solutions are often reachable. For instance, in 1989 the Montreal Protocol treaty banned ozone-depleting chlorofluorocarbons (popularly known as CFCs) worldwide. Similarly, the United States and other tuna-fishing countries reached an agreement in the 1990s about using dolphin-friendly fishing methods.

So the way ahead for environmental protections is clear, at least in principle: appropriately chosen policies can address externalities and common-pool resource problems. Countries' willingness to craft, implement, enforce, and pay for the inevitable cost of such policies increases as their incomes rise. This effect seems more pronounced in democracies than in authoritarian regimes (as in China, where the public increasingly demands environmental protections, but the government's response is spotty). Democracies tend to better protect private property rights, which encourage responsible, nonwasteful uses of environmental resources. (Few engines of environmental destruction are more powerful than an authoritarian state bent on making rapid progress in favored kinds of industrial or agricultural output.) Overall it is fair to conclude that growth and environmental protection are compatible. Income growth in general, and in democratic societies in particular, is linked to growing environmental protection and improvement.

That said, economic growth in many countries will put stress on the environment for a long time. Richer nations would be well advised to share clean technology with developing countries, offer education and policy advice to help those countries minimize damage to the environment, and hasten their progress along the EKC.

CRISES OF SUSTAINABILITY
The second type of environmental critique of growth focuses on sustainability. This critique holds that even if the world is making progress in controlling individual pollutants, modern economic life

has such a large footprint in the ecosphere that it threatens the fundamental, long-term sustainability of large, high-income human populations. In this view, the world faces two kinds of potential calamity. First, there are resource limits: we might literally run out of nonrenewable natural resources such as oil, minerals, and natural gas. Second, we may hit biological limits on human activity due to population growth and global warming, climate change, and loss of biodiversity; the argument is that limits on the energy and calories that can be extracted from the biosphere are likely to be felt suddenly and catastrophically. Concerns of this type are called "neo-Malthusian" after Reverend Thomas Malthus, who famously argued early in the 1800s that inexorable human population growth would outpace the rate of food production, leading to widespread death from famine and pestilence. Prominent exponents of neo-Malthusian arguments include Bill McKibben, Paul Ehrlich, Herman Daly, and former US vice president Al Gore, whose book (and movie) *An Inconvenient Truth* argues that the world is on the cusp of irreversible environmental catastrophe due to carbon dioxide–driven climate change.

Mainstream economists have argued consistently for decades that neo-Malthusians exaggerate the long-run effects of resource constraints—and there is a lot of evidence to support their contention. In real, inflation-adjusted terms, the prices of most nonrenewable commodities have drifted lower since World War II, strong evidence that resource constraints are not binding. "Proven reserves" of these commodities have ballooned, so that it is not uncommon today for reserve and annual consumption levels of a resource (such as copper) to be higher than they were one or two decades ago. The late economist Julian Simon, a prominent critic of neo-Malthusianism, won a famous bet against Paul Ehrlich when he correctly predicted that the prices of several commodities would fall, rather than rise, over a particular decade.

The near-consensus among mainstream economists that resource constraints can be overcome hinges on the nature of the price system and how proven reserves are measured. Commodity reserves are calculated as the amount of a resource it makes economic sense to extract, given current technologies and current prices. Proven reserve figures do not represent the actual total volume of a particular resource that exists; they are more like markers of what it is realistic to consider extracting, at a given moment in time. So, for instance, the development of new ways to drill sideways into shale (fracking) has unlocked vast new amounts of natural gas reserves in the United States. The United States consumed approximately 50 percent more natural gas between 1980 and 2010 than was estimated in 1979 to be in proven reserves.[28] The price system plays a critical role in directing an economy's response to resource constraints. Prices rise when demand for resources hits natural supply limits. On the supply side, price increases encourage technological change, searches for new sources of the commodity, and increased recycling; on the demand side, price increases induce more careful consumption and the search for substitutes. The evidence on this point is so strong that some neo-Malthusians have conceded the matter. As Bill McKibben puts it, Julian Simon has been proven right, "so far."[29]

McKibben's "so far" catches the other side of the neo-Malthusian argument—that continued economic growth may bring humanity to the biological limit of sustainability, with apocalyptic consequences. A scenario in which global carbon dioxide emissions cause global warming, which then triggers catastrophic events such as rising sea levels, disruption of the Gulf Stream, and loss of Arctic ice coverage, is of course the best example of this problem. Carbon emissions are not the only potential catalyst of crisis. Excessive water drawdowns from aquifers and excessive irrigation leading to irreversible salinization of agricultural land are among the many practices held to be pushing the planet toward a crisis.

Are we, in fact, at an environmental tipping point? It is hard to know for sure, but economists tend to doubt it. The measured rise in recent centuries of the atmosphere's carbon dioxide concentration is certainly due to man-made emissions. Its specific environmental consequences and their timing and magnitude are devilishly hard to pin down. Global warming poses a particularly complex common-pool resource problem. It is truly global in scope, which means that emissions reductions by even as large a carbon-emitting country as the United States cannot, alone, make a noticeable dent in global emissions trends. Virtually all large nations, rich and poor, would need to be part of a concerted effort to reduce carbon emissions in order to have an appreciable effect on trends in atmospheric carbon. Reining in greenhouse gas emissions is particularly costly compared to dealing with other global common-pool problems, because these emissions arise from virtually every kind of human activity. Thus global warming poses a kind of hyper-free-rider problem—no one wants to make painful steps first without the assurance that everyone is doing the same. Negotiating a solution will be extraordinarily difficult.

So what can be said about the effects of economic growth on environmental sustainability? First, purely biological models of limits to growth are inadequate for assessing possible outcomes and formulating policies. Human communities have the ability to innovate and adjust all kinds of policies in response to environmental challenges. They are capable of great sacrifice at times, but also of great creativity. Markets and the price system can direct and coordinate human responses very efficiently, helping good solutions emerge rapidly. Environmental catastrophe is not inevitable. Second, taking immediate and sweeping actions to forestall all *possible* environmental disasters is surely too aggressive a response to the uncertain consequences of global warming. Policies that promote economic growth will provide crucial financial resources to pay for modest (and perhaps increasingly strict) control of greenhouse gas emissions while also making progress toward other legitimate, pressing human needs such as poverty reduction.[30]

Policies to combat global warming should focus directly on the source of the problem, greenhouse gas emissions, rather than approaching the problem indirectly. This well-known efficiency principle in economics suggests that a broad-based global carbon tax, across all countries and all sources, would be best, because it would give all economic actors the incentive to reduce the use of carbon fuels in all activities. For instance, it would encourage the transition from coal-fired to natural gas–fired electric power plants, which would sharply cut greenhouse gas emissions (since the latter provide more energy with less carbon emissions). Other options to address carbon emissions are more expensive because they target the source of the problem less directly. For instance, taxing trade with countries that do not promote environmental sustainability might reduce shipping-related pollution, but in a particularly roundabout and therefore costly way. It would reduce income in rich and poor countries alike, while not necessarily helping poor countries adopt carbon-reducing technologies or specialize in clean industries. (Encouraging trade, by contrast, provides countries with funds to pay for ongoing improvements to emission controls.)

IN SUM

Growth causes pollution, but also provides the means and social willingness to reduce pollution; it is therefore better for the environment in the long run than poverty. Common-pool resources pose tricky, but not unsolvable, regulatory issues. These truths explain why progress has been made in environmental restoration in recent decades, and they undergird economists' view that economic growth is compatible with sustained environmental improvement. The details of environmental regulation matter a lot, because there are invariably less or more costly ways to achieve any given environmental goal. In general, approaches that are direct (rather than indirect) and market oriented will deliver the most cost-effective environmental protection. Because growth profoundly improves the welfare of the poor, it is a moral imperative not to be traded off too easily in the name of the environment.

5

OBJECTIONS TO GROWTH: CHARACTER AND COMMUNITY

The benefits of economic growth have been challenged on moral as well as environmental grounds. A wide range of social thinkers, including literary critics, moral philosophers, theologians, sociologists, and even economists themselves, have offered sweeping moral criticism of growth and progrowth policies. Many Christian thinkers are prominent among these critics. In their view, economic growth ignores the needs of the poor, and cultivates harmful personal attitudes of materialism and consumerism. In its incessant demand for change and improvement, growth degrades the quality of human communities. Rather than thinking of growth as a constructive response to scarcity, society should question the reality of scarcity itself and cultivate an ethic of sufficiency.

Many of these critiques are rooted, at bottom, in critiques of the moral legitimacy of markets. To assess them requires evaluating the morality of market economies. But to begin, it is worthwhile to consider the critiques in greater detail.

NEEDS VS. WANTS, SCARCITY VS. ABUNDANCE, AND COMMUNITIES VS. MARKETS

One objection to economic growth is that it distracts individuals and society from addressing genuine social needs. When those not in poverty desire a rising living standard, they are distracted from the needs of the truly hungry, "those who experience hunger as life-threatening deprivation."[31] Our individualistic material desires are cultivated by a marketplace geared to encouraging greater levels of self-satisfaction, pulling us away from addressing the claims of the truly needy. After all, as the Christian philosopher Kent Van Til suggests, the claims of the poor do not generate *"effective demand* that is recognized within the marketplace. The poor do not have the ability to pay the price asked by the market. Hence the market doesn't respond to their needs, but only satisfies the wants of those with sufficient income."[32] According to this view, the needs of the poor are ignored in market economies oriented toward producing greater output merely to satisfy rising wants.

Van Til's comment opens up a second objection to growth: that what individuals perceive to be economic "needs" are in fact socially constructed wants, stoked by advertising and other means of selfish persuasion. From this point of view, the concept of scarcity—which economists take to be a fundamental problem for the social order to address—is actually a symptom of an improperly organized and incorrectly viewed market system. Thus trying to satisfy economic needs through economic growth is seen as deeply problematic. Theologian Douglas Meeks asserts that by placing the satisfaction of needs at the fulcrum of the economy, modern economic theory and modern market economies pave the way for the pursuit of economic growth as a goal, since "needs are not limited and satiable but in principle unlimited and insatiable."[33] According to Meeks, "Growth should not be based on infinite needs and acquisition leading to an ever-widening appropriation of nature for the sake of accumulating wealth as power."[34]

This particular critique is widely shared among growth's critics. Theologian William Cavanaugh writes that "the idea of scarcity assumes that the normal condition for the communication of goods is through trade: to get something, one must relinquish something else. The idea of scarcity implies that goods are not held in common, that the consumption of goods is essentially a private experience."[35] The concept of scarcity itself is contingent on accepting the legitimacy of private property rights. In turn, private production is motivated by economic gain to satisfy wants, and the satisfaction of wants requires production via employment of laborers who are paid market wages. Mocking this "miracle of the market," Cavanaugh suggests that the story of the benefits of market-based resource allocation is a kind of "contemporary loaves-and-fishes saga" of "scarcity miraculously turned into abundance by consumption itself."[36]

Economist Bob Goudzwaard joins the chorus of skepticism about scarcity and need, contending that through the mass media there has been a "commercially promoted explosion of human needs in our already-rich societies."[37] The result has been an increase in scarcity, for "e-commerce and advertising campaigns push the level of human needs and desires artificially beyond the level of their possible saturation."[38] Goudzwaard calls on modern societies to take a lesson from the tree, which by (literally) organic self-restraint, ends its vertical growth at maturity, "in order to use its reserves fully to bear fruit and produce seeds."[39] Likewise, business firms, labor unions, and consumers ought to practice cooperation out of a spirit of self-restraint and contentment without pursuing economic growth as an end in itself.

A third critique is that growth harms local communities. Wendell Berry, long an advocate of the value of local community, challenges economic growth for eroding the local economies that are its basis.[40] Berry affirms that simple living with reliance on locally produced commodities acquired through personal exchange is most consistent with a "Great Economy" that puts work and material goods in their proper perspective. As a Christian, Berry argues that his perspective matches the demands of God, but his views find a sympathetic home across many religious and nonreligious observers. Berry is not concerned about productivity gains from scale economies and the greater extent of a market. In fact, he views the large corporations that are necessary to take advantage of scale, with their far-flung economic activities, as corrupt, monopolistic, largely unconstrained actors bent on little but power and profit. They certainly do not care what happens to communities, especially small ones, whose prosperity may be broken at any moment by a corporate move or policy change.

Not all critics of growth go to an antimarket extreme.[41] But many are dismayed at the intense focus on short-term growth that characterizes much discussion about the economy in market systems. News reports hang breathlessly on governments' quarterly announcements and revisions of GDP growth rates. More than 70 percent of all demand for goods and services in a typical wealthy country is demand for consumption goods and services, which means that consumption really does matter for growth and employment. This fact, according to growth's critics, is a ready rationale for materialism, for short-sighted, debt-financed consumption today rather than prudential saving for the future, or (as noted Christian critic of capitalism Jim Wallis puts it) for outright idolatry and mammon worship.[42] It is no wonder that people can think that the United States and other countries have a "growth fetish" and are obsessed with growth at all costs. And a closely related concern is that by its emphasis on satisfying *present* consumer wants, economic growth taps resources not available to future generations. Surely, critics claim, economic growth is hardly ever optimal in its provision for the future.

ASSESSING THE CRITICISM

These critiques contain elements of truth. The critics are right to fear that a growing abundance of goods and services may lead individuals to place their trust in wealth for their security. (Christians should name such a tendency as idolatrous and challenge it.) The critics are also right to be concerned about how growth and the market economy affect values and morality. And they are right to value community. But they miss crucial features of how economic life and morality truly affect one another. Most fundamentally, their views misjudge the full extent of the benefits of growth for rich and poor countries, benefits that can assist moral development. They also misattribute genuine moral problems (materialism, lack of concern for the poor) to growth and to the market rather than thinking of them as inherent in free human communities. Hence they fail to see that these problems are best countered by healthy culture and virtue rather than slower growth.

Although critics of growth do not acknowledge them, the material benefits of growth for poor economies—and poor people—are undeniable. As we showed in chapter 2, the very low levels of income in much of the poor world today mean that redistribution would simply result in shared poverty. Growth offers the only avenue to sustained improvements in material well-being. The most common moral concerns about growth—that it distracts attention from real social needs, that it constantly creates new "needs," or that it harms local communities—are not relevant to the poor, for whom growth may mean not only higher incomes but clean water, publicly provided education, and accessible health care. Rebecca Blank, a prominent US poverty analyst, acutely observes, "For most people throughout history, 'simple living' has meant subsistence farming," which sadly translates into "involuntary rural poverty."[43]

Moral concerns about growth are relevant to rich countries; but these countries also experience real and substantial benefits from growth. Even a society where per capita income is already above $50,000 per year can benefit from more income. There is no lack of good ends to which our society could apply billions of dollars of fresh resources available only from growth. The ongoing fights against cancer and Alzheimer's disease, for instance, require labs and skilled medical caregivers and researchers. Ongoing work to reduce pollution of all kinds requires research and investments in every industry. (These efforts raise life expectancy, a big benefit of economic growth even for rich countries.) The ongoing challenge of providing good education through college, postgraduate study, or vocational training requires resources, skilled personnel, and capital. The ongoing creation of new products that meet real needs requires billions in research and development expenditures. (Just a quarter century ago, there were no cell phones; today, who would be eager to live without them? Or without the Internet?) Ongoing improvements in travel that take international mobility and global understanding to new levels require substantial investments in infrastructure. These are all genuine needs—the meeting of which are genuine goods—and not mere wants. The fact that obtaining them requires investment of time, money, and effort means that scarcity is real, not imaginary.

GROWTH AND MORALITY

But does material prosperity provide moral benefits? Can it really be better than poverty in anything other than a gross material sense? Yes—though reaping those benefits takes thoughtful work by citizens and governments.

Economists have long known that certain kinds of moral norms can assist economic growth by, say, buttressing the legitimacy of private property. But economists and other social thinkers also suggest that economic growth itself fosters several kinds of positive moral outcomes. Thus Joel Mokyr has it right in arguing that during the British Industrial Revolution, a complex, two-way relationship between norms and economic growth was at work. He writes that in eighteenth-century Britain, growth was grounded in "the pre-existence of certain social norms and cooperative behavior and a voluntary willingness to forego opportunistic behavior that made transactions, even at arm's length, possible."[44] These directly promoted commercialization, "which brought about economic growth through gains from trade."[45] He adds that without an understanding of "how property rights were increasingly respected and contracts honored (rather than enforced), we will miss something about the institutional roots of subsequent economic growth."[46] Thus, for instance, the development of credit markets required credible behavior or reputation that the merchant/tradesman acquired over time by his industry, integrity, and other good qualities, and that were in turn encouraged by the growing market system.[47]

Writing during the first stage of the Industrial Revolution, Adam Smith argued in the *Wealth of*

Nations that commercialization encourages improved moral character. As living standards rise where markets are allowed to expand, probity thrives and deceit is suppressed, because the value of a good personal reputation and the rewards from being able to collaborate in business with people outside of one's family are so much bigger than before. The market also encourages such virtuous habits as planning for the future, taking responsibility for one's livelihood, and thinking independently.

This argument is as relevant today as it was in Smith's era. Britain may have been the first country to experience the Industrial Revolution, but the same moral trends will be evident in any country that puts growth on a market footing. Twentieth- and twenty-first-century observers point to a variety of ways in which economic growth and markets encourage virtuous behavior. Francis Fukuyama, for instance, argues that generalized social trust is the most valuable element of social capital and growth, and that markets encourage it even as they depend on it.[48] Benjamin Friedman likewise claims that economic growth leads to moral improvement because it not only strongly encourages greater tolerance of others' economic success but also makes members of society less tolerant of prejudices (legal or informal) that restrict opportunity and economic mobility.[49] By contrast, a stagnant economy is plagued by harmful moral consequences. For example, when most find their incomes declining, those individuals who do manage to get ahead are perceived not only as doing so at other people's expense but as directly disadvantaging others. Suspicions rise regarding the accumulation of wealth from the productive use of capital. And a greater intensity of resentment leads to intolerance, lack of generosity, and less willingness to trust others, all of which undermine the foundations of democracy and of successful market institutions.[50]

The fact that markets and growth promote probity, honesty, and other "commercial" virtues (a term not always meant as a compliment) strikes some critics as at best a weak defense of markets. Should not society want a more robust cultivation of virtue, for its own sake, not materially motivated? Yes. But neither should this feature of markets and growth be taken lightly. Alternative nonmarket or state-dominated systems, likely to put much greater limits on economic liberty, cannot be expected to do a better job of encouraging citizens to practice the commercial virtues—or other virtues.

Christian thought suggests several additional positive moral aspects of economic growth and the markets and other institutions that sustain it. They spring from the Christian view that the material world is fundamentally good, that humans are called to "tend the earth and keep it" (Genesis 3:15), and that humans are made in God's image (that is, in the image of a creator God, Genesis 1:27). These beliefs imply that poverty is not God's desired state for humanity. Prosperity, honestly obtained, is good—though it should never be thought of as an expected benefit of faith. Material well-being that is the result of human creativity, investment, and work should be celebrated, not shunned—though wealth is never to be worshipped in place of God. Environmental stewardship and care for the earth are goods—but not the only goods. Though fallen due to sin, humans retain the image of God and thus have a kind of intrinsic goodness that makes them worthy of care, too. Individuals have an inalienable dignity that requires institutions that respect their freedom of action and the legitimacy of their command over resources, even as those individuals are called to make wise decisions about their time, talents, and responsibilities. These are the enduring foundations on which a healthy growth ethic can be built. The Christian worldview puts the material world into balanced perspective, wanting neither to be a slave to growth nor fearful of embracing it.

THE CHARACTER OF GROWTH IN RICH ECONOMIES
People in poor economies come naturally to a clear-eyed view of the merits of growth. By contrast, in

rich societies, the case for growth is less obvious. Growth needs to be held in mind consciously as a morally legitimate policy goal, lest it die a death of a thousand cuts from the cumulative effect of many small policy choices that erode it in the name of other good ends. To sustain growth, national policies must support and nurture the personal (and civic) virtues of truth telling, public-spiritedness, and self-sacrifice, along with courage, love, and prudence.

Goudzwaard's metaphor of the economy as a tree—knowing organically when to stop growing, and functioning best at stable maturity—is inadequate for thinking about a rich economy. While a sense of sufficiency is excellent practice for individuals (who are indeed wise to reject greed and who should follow their callings, be they lucrative or not), it is not appropriate for a nation or an economy as a whole to cease growing. Indeed, far from being organic, cessation of growth for the entire human community would be unnatural—it would be the result of constraints on creativity, freedom, and stewardship.

Pursuing the path of growth, properly framed, offers the best response to arguments like Berry's about community and location. It is precisely in a wealthy market-based economy that people can enjoy local food and organic products, because they can afford the intrinsically higher cost of those goods. Satisfying a propensity to foster community by purchasing higher-priced local products is a legitimate part of human flourishing. The point is that a local economy should not be regulated into existence (what kinds of draconian laws would that require—bans on transporting blueberries across state lines?) but should rather emerge spontaneously from individuals' choices. Society and individuals, in short, must recognize the benefits of wide choice and leisure time that spring from economic growth grounded in markets and productivity gains. As Rebecca Blank puts it, these are benefits "which allow us to use more effectively the diverse skills that we have been given as human beings by our Creator."[51]

Fortunately, growth in a market economy need not hinge on materialism. Here good economics dovetails with good morality in a particularly helpful way. Materialistic, short-sighted consumer behavior is worth critiquing; neither markets nor economic growth requires that people act in such a way. The US economy's emphasis on consumption over savings in recent decades reflects misplaced federal and state spending priorities and unwise tax incentives of various kinds, among many other things, rather than the fundamental character of economic growth in the short or long term.

Though spending on goods and services really does influence the level of employment, there is nothing about economic growth per se that requires spending on tawdry consumption items rather than on investing in productive assets like education and housing and in valuable services like health care. If US consumers save more, a healthy financial system can translate those savings into investment spending by large and small firms. Economic growth and growth in employment would continue, but on a firmer footing. But of course, only a culture that consistently endorses the virtues of human dignity, self-control, prudence, and honesty, and that fosters an orientation toward the future rather than present self-gratification and self-indulgence, will allow us to make this transition and best harness the fruits of growth.

IN SUM

Moral critics of economic growth point to social and spiritual dangers associated with it, including materialism, neglect of the poor due to a selfish focus on satisfying one's one desires, and the undermining of local communities. These claims severely underestimate the wide range of material benefits economic growth provides across income levels. They also fail to acknowledge the connection, in market economies, between growth and moral goods such as social trust, honesty, compassion, and taking responsibility for oneself and one's family. These economies both depend on these values and help to generate them. Where economic growth is stymied, envy and uncharitable behavior spread.

Those who identify with the Christian faith have strong reasons to encourage economic freedom and equality of opportunity, which both promote and are sustained by growth. A Christian worldview regards the material benefits of growth, honestly obtained, as the opportunity to enjoy God's bountiful creation and to serve others.

Societies' moral failures should be attributed neither to economic growth nor to markets. Rather, growth helps people address the human failures that are bound to arise in free societies.

6

GROWTH AND GOVERNMENT FINANCE

Governments have income (from taxes) and spend it (on social welfare programs, national defense, and other needs). Just as families sometimes struggle to balance income and spending (for reasons of their own making, or because of things beyond their control), governments can run into trouble with their finances. When that happens, it is usually due to unwise policy choices about taxes, spending, and borrowing; less frequently, it is for reasons beyond that nation's control.

One part of the economic case for growth has to do with its close connection to government finances: governments' decisions about taxes and spending have a major impact on economic growth. Faster growth can be very beneficial to a nation's finances; but growth itself, and therefore national welfare, can be deeply threatened if a nation's finances are not in order. To explain, we first define terms. The government runs a *deficit* when it spends more than it receives in tax revenue. A *budget surplus* occurs when spending is less than tax revenue, a rare situation. Over the years, the US federal government, like most other governments, has regularly run budget deficits. In the United States before 1960, budget deficits occurred mostly in times of war, but since the mid-1960s they have been a persistent feature of the economy. Deficits must be financed by borrowing, so a nation's total debt rises when there is a deficit; a budget surplus lowers debt.

GROWTH HELPS FINANCES—AND SOFTENS INTERGENERATIONAL CONFLICT

Consider the good news first. Growth helps national finances directly and powerfully. Faster growth means higher tax revenues, because more people are working and paying taxes, and more people are in higher tax brackets. Therefore, the government can spend less on safety-net programs (food stamps, welfare, unemployment compensation) than it would in times of lower employment and income levels. Thus deficits fall and might even turn to surpluses. Growth produced surpluses in the late 1990s, when the US economy grew at an unusually fast pace and the government ran four years of budget surpluses. (The previous surplus had been in 1969.) For the United States, this growth effect is big. The Office of Management and Budget estimates that each additional percentage point of growth in GDP in a given year lowers the federal budget deficit by $72 billion per year (on average) over the ensuing ten years. That is equal to about half a percent of GDP.[52]

This feature of growth is helpful for all countries. Poor countries have pressing needs for government-assisted health and education programs, agricultural extension services, infrastructure development, and pollution control. High growth combined with appropriate taxes and wise spending choices by government can turbocharge human welfare improvements. Rich countries face demographic pressures in the form of rapidly aging populations. Economic growth over the next several decades would help the United States, Japan, and European countries fund their pay-as-you-go retirement programs (such as Social Security and Medicare).

Let us consider the United States in particular. A dramatic shift is underway in the ratio of people age sixty-five or older to people of working age (twenty to sixty-four). That ratio has been approximately 20 percent (or a little lower) since the 1970s, but it will surge to 35 percent between 2010 and the mid-2030s and is projected to stay at that level through the 2080s. Instead of more than five workers' taxes sustaining each retiree's Social Security payment, there will be fewer than three. Through 2010, Social Security taxes raised more money than was needed to make Social Security payments to eligible individuals. The excess was placed in the Social Security Trust Fund, held in the form of Treasury bonds; now, the government is drawing down the fund to pay retirees. If Social Security benefits, tax rates, or eligibility criteria are not changed, the trust fund will be exhausted in 2033. At that point, the payable benefits will be limited to the amount of funds collected, meaning that benefits will effectively suffer a massive 25 percent cut, equivalent to 1.5 percent of GDP.[53] The looming funding problem for Medicare is even worse. To maintain these programs' payments unchanged would require punishingly large extra taxes on younger people.

Europe and Japan face similar demographic challenges, and because they have had lower birth rates for longer, they may reach a crisis sooner than the United States. China also faces this problem because of its coercive "one child" population control policy. One way to gauge the size of the looming problem is to ask how large a tax increase would be needed to fund existing government transfer payment obligations. In Japan, future generations would face a 25 percent increase in total taxes; in the Netherlands, 22 percent; in Germany, 14 percent.[54] Tax increases (or benefit cuts) on this scale would be politically and economically difficult to digest, to put it mildly.

Higher income growth can smooth out many of these difficulties. It simplifies every aspect of adjusting to an aging population. It gives countries resources to invest so money will be on hand later to pay benefits in future years. If changes must be made, higher growth allows governments to make smaller cuts to benefits, to rely more heavily on private pensions (whose funding prospers when growth is higher) and, if necessary, to raise taxes a smaller amount, than they would otherwise. One credible estimate is that, for the United States, growth at 2.6 percent a year on average between 2010 and 2035 leaves net government debt at 155 percent of GDP. Growth at only 1.0 percent would burden the economy with net government debt of 302 percent of GDP.[55] Higher growth is an essential element of solving the West's fiscal problems and avoiding intergenerational conflict.

DEBT AND DEFICITS THREATEN GROWTH

Even casual observers of the US federal government are aware that its budget deficit has grown to gargantuan proportions in recent years. In fiscal years 2009 through 2012, the federal budget deficit has ranged from 7 to 10 percent of GDP, greater than in any year since 1946 and the end of World War II. By early 2012, the cumulative effect of these deficits pushed total federal debt higher than all of US GDP (more than $15 trillion), the first time since World War II that the United States has been in this unenviable position.

Economic growth and government budgets deficits are closely connected, with cause and effect working two ways. If the government runs a large budget deficit, the growth rate of the economy can be lower than it otherwise would have been. On the other hand, if economic growth is low, or even negative, the government's budget deficit can increase automatically.

The detailed explanation goes like this: during a recession, when economic growth slows down and perhaps becomes negative (causing total income to fall), the government's budget deficit automatically increases. Falling incomes yield lower tax revenue, while at the same time the government must increase spending on safety-net programs. In response to a recession, governments also typically increase spending and reduce tax rates to create additional demand for goods and services. The Obama administration sought to speed up recovery from the 2008 recession, for instance, by increasing government spending by $787 billion in 2009 (the "stimulus package") and by cutting the Social Security payroll tax by two percentage points in 2011. The automatic increase in the budget deficit combined with the discretionary stimulus may yield short-term benefits. Growth in demand leads to increased production (or a smaller decrease in production than would otherwise occur), though this effect is questioned by many economists.[56] What is certain, however, is that the deficit rises from both the automatic and the discretionary spending increases.

How do budget deficits and a growing national debt at this present large scale affect the rate of growth? Any increase in the budget deficit forces the government to borrow additional funds in financial markets. This increase in borrowing causes interest rates to rise (all else equal). Consequently, other borrowers—such as businesses seeking funds to finance expansion or the purchase of new capital (for example, machines, computers or delivery trucks), or households seeking mortgages (to purchase homes)—will incur higher costs. These higher interest costs will discourage some firms and households from spending on new capital. This is called "crowding out." Government borrowing ends up reducing private investment, which in turn reduces overall growth in the economy.

There is solid evidence that the effect of deficit borrowing on interest rates is large. Everything else equal, a sustained 1 percent increase in the budget deficit as a share of GDP raises long-term interest rates by 1 to 1.5 percentage points, even in an economy as large and internationally integrated as the United States (which can borrow capital from around the world).[57] So we can conclude that a large US deficit going forward will inhibit capital formation and lower growth. The same can be said for virtually any country, rich or poor.

Since 2008, however, the US economy has

been in a recession (or slow recovery). The central bank (in the United States, the Federal Reserve) has chosen to use monetary policy to lower interest rates in an effort to stimulate borrowing and spending by businesses and households. This choice offsets, to some extent, the crowding-out effect discussed above, though at the cost of greatly expanding the money supply. (If large enough, this will cause inflation, for the simple reason that more money "chases" existing goods and services.) When combined with increased deficit spending by the government, lower interest rates make growing government debt seem cheaper than it really will prove to be in the long run. In the case of the United States, the Federal Reserve's low-interest/easy-money policy has been aggressively followed for so long that by some measures the money supply appears to have tripled since the onset of the financial crisis. This means that the potential inflationary problem when economic growth resumes in earnest is also very large.

Small deficits, and small total debt as a share of GDP, may be sustainable indefinitely. But a large debt relative to GDP sets the stage for a nasty problem: a fiscal crisis. A fiscal crisis occurs when lenders become worried about a government's ability to meet its debt obligations, and begin to fear that the government may end up in default.

Such worries have recently plagued Greece, Spain, Italy, and Ireland. When these concerns emerge, they result immediately in higher interest rates on government borrowing. At their worst, they can lead to a self-fulfilling "death spiral" for an economy, in which worries about the government's ability to pay its creditors cause interest rates to rise, which makes it more expensive to pay down debt, which raises fears that the government may default, which raises interest rates.

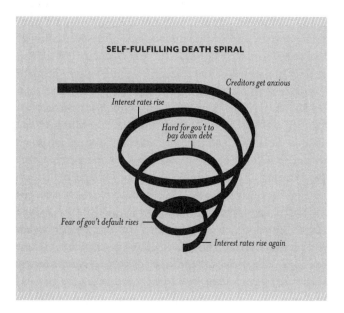

SELF-FULFILLING DEATH SPIRAL

Creditors get anxious

Interest rates rise

Hard for gov't to pay down debt

Fear of gov't default rises

Interest rates rise again

It is sobering to realize that with a total government debt exceeding GDP, the United States is in territory that for many other nations has yielded a fiscal crisis. The United States retains certain advantages—for instance, its government debt is safer than debts of most other countries, so it benefits from being a safe haven for lenders—but the fact is that if US debt continues to grow as a share of GDP, the United States very well could have a fiscal crisis. None of the options in a fiscal crisis is attractive. A country must either default, arrange debt write-downs with its creditors (who may demand painful spending cuts), or engage in inflationary finance (basically, print more money). All of these options hurt a country, leaving it poorer and in deep recession.[58] It takes years for growth and income to recover.

DEFICITS, INFLATION, AND ECONOMIC GROWTH

A further problem that government deficits and debt pose for growth relates to inflation. As noted earlier, governments almost everywhere run budget deficits. Deficits are the norm, not the exception. When deficits and debts are small relative to GDP, crowding out is small and fiscal crises are avoided, so the debt may be sustainable indefinitely, assuming that the government can borrow funds at reasonable interest rates. This last condition is crucial and is not met in many poor countries.

In the United States, citizens take it for granted that a government can borrow from the public if it needs funds. This practice has no effect on the money supply, because the government is borrowing funds that already exist. But in many poor countries, financial markets are undeveloped, or the government is not trustworthy, or both, so it is not possible to borrow from the public. If a government cannot borrow it has three choices: increase taxes, reduce spending, or print money. The government may fear negative political fallout from the first two choices, so a typical choice is to print money to finance its spending. But printing money has consequences. Increases in the money supply over and above the rate of real output growth cause prices to rise—that is, it creates inflation. This result is called an inflation tax, because the government in effect relies on a decrease in the purchasing power of the currency to cover its budget deficit.

Many poor countries have resorted to the inflation tax. It is one of the main reasons why developing-country inflation rates since the 1950s have almost always been higher than inflation in developed countries. Indeed, as a rule of thumb, any country with a sustained inflation rate of greater than 10 percent per year is likely suffering from the inflation tax. Inflation at this level or higher almost always harms growth. It muddies price signals, making it hard for people to identify low-cost inputs and the most cost-efficient actions. Consumers and businesses find it increasingly difficult to budget and plan future spending as the prices of products and resources rise unevenly. Unless interest rates are allowed to rise to levels higher than the inflation rate, people hesitate to save in banks, and borrowers get funds far more cheaply than they should—so savings fall and capital gets wasted. In the extreme, the inflation tax causes hyperinflation, as occurred in Zimbabwe in the early 2000s; inflation hit 489 billion percent, and average incomes crashed.[59] When it comes to designing institutions to secure growth, economists to a person recommend independent central banks so that political pressure to run the inflation tax can be resisted.

IN SUM

Growth helps government finances directly and immediately, but mismanaged finances can seriously hurt growth and thus the public welfare. Countries like the United States that face large unfunded spending obligations need to make certain that they are growing at a healthy rate. Growth softens the fiscal burden of spending obligations; in particular, a key moral benefit of growth is that it eases what could otherwise be very painful intergenerational conflict between the young and the old about promised government social spending. For rich and poor countries alike, fiscal crises and the inflation tax have harmful, potentially severe, consequences for growth.

7

SECURING GROWTH: CRUCIAL POLICY QUESTIONS AND CHOICES

Chapter 2 identified as sources of sustainable economic growth the institutions that provide individuals and firms with significant incentives to invest in physical and human capital, and to innovate. In this chapter we examine those institutions closely and seek to answer a variety of questions about the policy choices connected to them, including what economic institutions and policy choices are best for promoting economic growth, whether growth policies look different in rich and poor countries, whether democracy really is necessary or helpful for growth, and what kinds of international economic arrangements boost growth.

DOMESTIC POLICIES

The institutions that promote accumulation and innovation make for a short list. Simply stated, they are an impartial judicial system committed to the rule of law, to the protection of private property, and to the security of economic transactions; a stable government free of corruption that can provide for national defense and other public goods; a market system for the production and distribution of most goods and services; and a functional financial system with a sound currency, to encourage savings and efficient investments.

Below we recommend the institutions and policies that represent a kind of "gold standard" for encouraging growth. There is strong empirical evidence that each one helps long-run growth, though few countries come close to hitting all of these ideals.

To encourage growth, a country should have an independent judiciary within a constitutionally governed system that respects civil rights, the principle of equality before the law, and the legitimacy of private property rights. The national government should opt for low, stable corporate and income tax rates, applied broadly to all sources of income or to expenditure. The government should offer few subsidies, focusing its spending instead on providing genuine public goods (such as national defense, national health campaigns, or basic research and development) that cannot be adequately supplied by private firms. There should be very little outright state ownership of industry—the private sector can make investment decisions better than the government, and state-owned firms inevitably get captured by special interests (for example, unions, government bureaucracies, or some other faction).

Social spending should be focused on health and education to equip people with human capital, the key personal endowment necessary for wealth building. Much of this spending should be means tested to focus it on the poor rather than rich, and structured in ways that partner with—rather than replace—the private sector. For instance, in education, private schools should be encouraged (under reasonable regulation); state-run schools or state-funded scholarships for poor families can then supplement private-sector efforts without requiring the government to become a monopoly education provider.

Barriers to trade should be minimal—there should be low tariffs, few quotas, and no restrictions on access to foreign exchange. This arrangement is essential for gaining trade's considerable growth advantages. Trade allows specialization and economies of scale in producing for global markets. Firms and countries engaged in trade grow faster and learn more than when growth comes from the domestic market alone. Furthermore, trade protection imposes high penalties on exporters and the poor, both of whom benefit from access to less expensive products from abroad.

Finally, the financial system—commercial and investment banks, insurance companies, and other financial firms—must be allowed to do its crucial job of pooling funds from savers to lend for investments. The central bank should be politically independent of the treasury so monetary policy is used for no goal other than long-term price stability. While financial systems need regulation, too much regulation, or domination by the state, will harm growth. State-dominated systems feature large state-owned banks and interest-rate restrictions; these banks often pay below-market interest rates to depositors while being required to lend at below-market rates to favored borrowers. Inevitably, this combination of practices reduces savings and wastes capital on unproductive projects.

When a poor country's government commits to catch-up growth and makes a decisive break with growth-killing socialist or statist policies, only a few items from the ideal policy menu need be adopted before rapid growth ignites. China's decisive economic liberalization in 1978 occurred with the adoption of the household responsibility system in agriculture. Farmers, who previously had been treated as (badly paid) wage labor on communes, were allowed to pay fixed, in-kind rent for their land, keeping for themselves any production in excess of the rent. In essence, farmers regained a modest property right in their own output. Agricultural productivity exploded. Trade liberalization began in the mid-1980s, and trade and foreign direct investment very quickly became key drivers of rapid growth. Rules against private ownership of capital were slowly lifted, and private firms began to grow into the powerful force they are today. Yet, even now, more than three decades after market-oriented reform began, some key institutional and policy reforms have either not begun or not been completed. State-owned firms dominate many industries, and state-owned banks have a chokehold on commercial finance and savings while hiding mountains of bad debt under the skirts of their protected status. Firms that would otherwise go bankrupt, freeing resources to move to more productive uses, are kept afloat by the soft budget constraint of government funding. The rule of law and protection of property rights are imperfect at best.

India made its decisive move toward growth in 1991 with trade policy liberalization. But many severe labor market restrictions that make it difficult to expand and invest in manufacturing remain in place. (For instance, large manufacturing firms generally cannot fire workers.) Thus the service sector has driven India's growth, not low-skilled manufacturing.

Poor countries thus have considerable ability to achieve catch-up growth without implementing a full set of market-oriented institutions. But in the long term, there is no substitute for these institutions. Entrepreneurs need to be freed from legal shackles that discourage them from taking risks in starting new businesses.[60] When economic actors cannot securely hold, transfer, and receive income from property, growth is stifled. And, tellingly, state control over large portions of the economy proves increasingly expensive as growth proceeds. The easy, high-productivity investments are exhausted. As some industries get closer to the cutting edge, state economic planners will make big investment mistakes. State-dominated financial systems can neither funnel credit to deserving small businesses nor escape the insatiable demands of money-losing state firms. Increasingly, wealthy citizens will bridle at being forced to save at low interest rates in state-owned banks and find ways to send their savings outside the country for higher returns (legally or illegally).

The challenges of building the wider set of institutions necessary to sustain growth when catch-up growth approaches its natural limits sometimes create what economists call the "middle-income trap." This is a moment when a rapidly growing economy, hitting middle income, finds that its real per capita growth rate drops substantially. Historically, this occurs around a per capita income of $16,000 (in 2005 international dollars), though there is considerable variation from country to country.[61]

Countries can avoid the trap by continuing to liberalize and move toward some version of the full set of institutions sketched above. Basically, countries need to rebalance the sources of growth and move from reliance on capital and labor accumulation to reliance on technological change and innovation. That change is not easy. It requires progress on all institutional and policy fronts. Governments themselves often need deep reforms when they "are themselves an important threat to the security of property rights and a prime violator of contracts."[62] China, for instance, is approaching middle income. To sustain rapid growth, it will need to strengthen the rule of law and property rights—a challenge for an authoritarian regime. But this step is necessary to protect the intellectual property that will become a major driver of China's next growth phase. It is also necessary to protect the rights of farmers to use land without fear of arbitrary takings by officials, which has debilitated large-scale agricultural investment. The financial system will need to be reformed to allow large private banks that can operate at arm's length from the government. China and other middle-income countries will likely find these changes challenging, but the social consensus that economic growth is an essential national aspiration will help them navigate passage through them.

Rich countries also face issues in maintaining their cutting-edge growth. They come closer to having the full set of "gold standard" institutions for growth than do poor countries, but they struggle to maintain them. Demands for social spending put inexorable upward pressure on tax rates, while beneficiaries of special-interest tax breaks hamper progress toward expanding the tax base. (Think of the US mortgage interest tax deduction.) Exploding deficits and debt, as discussed in chapter 6, pose real threats to growth. In the United States, demand for universal health care is testing our traditional aversion to coercive government control over intimate aspects of individuals' lives. In addition to making difficult judgments about the trade-offs between taxes and spending, rich-country citizens will need to think clearly about the consequences for growth of future policy choices. It is essential that they understand the extent to which growth is a means of human flourishing, so that its benefits are not traded away too readily for lesser goods.

POLITICAL INSTITUTIONS AND ECONOMIC GROWTH

Economic growth is inextricably tied to politics. Policy choices are political choices, and economic growth empowers newly wealthy groups to make political demands. One basic question about growth is its connection to specific political choices—that is, are democracy and civil liberties necessary for economic growth, or can promarket autocrats secure property rights and innovation, thereby stimulating economic growth? Conversely, does economic growth spur democratization?

History and research suggest some answers. Economic growth can begin and continue for a considerable time in undemocratic states. Chapter 2 noted the potential for autocratic regimes to fall into a resource trap, locking countries into low-growth paths. Yet, in some cases, a narrow elite tolerates and encourages more inclusive institutions, and economic growth may ensue, as in the case of South Korea and Taiwan in the 1950s through the 1980s.[63] Neither country had large deposits of valuable natural resources, and both faced a pressing external military threat. These factors led them to create institutions that were wealth generating, rather than merely appropriating existing streams of wealth for themselves.

South Korea and Taiwan serve as hopeful examples of how growth and the institutions that promote it can encourage democratization and the adoption of full civil rights. Both countries are now full-fledged democracies. In each country, income growth itself equipped people with knowledge about, and resources to press for, democratic governance. And the institutions that help to promote growth—such as a judiciary and a legal system committed to the rule of law, private firms and institutions not entirely beholden to the state, and a press able to report events honestly—turned out to be equally helpful in promoting democracy. If democratic governance and civil rights not only are considered intrinsically valuable but also are valuable for cultivating the habits of thoughtful civic engagement necessary to sustain healthy government and business institutions, then growth's effects on governance are a key part of the moral case for growth.

SECURING GROWTH: THE ROLE OF TRADE

Any evaluation of how to secure growth must also address the orientation of international economic institutions. Small countries find the gains to specialization and exchange compellingly large and cannot entertain any notions of growth and development outside of global integration. To put this starkly: could a small country like, say, Taiwan, ever prosper if it were to try to make most of its own steel, chemicals, pharmaceuticals, aircraft, oil, natural gas, textiles and apparel, education, and food? To ask this question is to answer it. Even continental-sized economies like the United States and India find it hard to grow without being deeply integrated into the global economy, given the size of gains from specialization and exchange.

What kinds of international economic institutions best sustain the deep international integration that nourishes growth? To answer this question, it is instructive to consider the multilateral effort to construct an open (rather than restrictive) global trading system following World War II. With European and Japanese support, the United States led the development of the treaty system governing trade that culminated in 1995 in the creation of the World Trade Organization (WTO). The system was dedicated to progressive trade liberalization among members through successive rounds of multilateral trade negotiations, and to rules-based adjudication of trade disputes. It has, in large part, succeeded in these aims. The most recent (Doha) round of negotiations has hit a stalemate, but for reasons that are symptomatic of its success: reaching a consensus on the best next steps for global trade liberalization is difficult when there are more than 150 members crowding into the negotiations, and when the issues that remain are the hardest ones, relating to trade in services and agriculture.

There can be no question that the success of the WTO system contributed to the growth that poor and rich countries alike have experienced since the 1940s. Countries have been encouraged to adopt open trade policies because they have seen successful examples in operation and, crucially, because the WTO offers assurance that other partner nations will be committed through binding treaty obligations to the maintenance of such policies.

There is an important element of justice in the practice of rich countries keeping markets open not just for their own economic well-being but also for the sake of growth in poorer countries. Rich countries have many ways to help their own lower-skilled citizens and any others who might be harmed by trade in the short term, and they need not resort to giving them trade-protected jobs at great harm to poverty reduction in the rest of the world.

IN SUM

The institutions necessary for sustained growth are the well-known institutions of a market economy and private property. This is not to say that these institutions are easy to develop and the associated policies easy to choose. Both may require courageous political leadership, a process assisted when societies understand the merits of market-oriented institutions and progrowth policies. Policy choices need not be the same in every country; growth can succeed in multiple ways within a basic market orientation. The market-oriented economic policies that support growth are deeply consistent with human freedom and political democracy. Human rights and economic growth may develop in tandem or unevenly, but they fundamentally support one another.

Internationally, growth may require champions of openness to make sure that an open, rules-based system remains in place. The United States for many years led by example: despite instances of trade protection, the United States gradually reduced trade barriers to their present historically low levels. How China chooses to act over the next decades will have a big impact on global growth prospects. If it, too, is willing to lead toward openness by example, it will help the next generation of growing economies; if not, its protectionism will complicate, though not stop, the process of growth in the rest of the world.

8

CONCLUSION: GROWTH'S PROMISE

There is a strong case for human flourishing based on sustained economic growth, for rich and poor countries alike. Indeed, the core proposition of this book is that growth is a moral issue because of its impact on the flourishing—or shriveling—of human society. The neglect of growth has moral consequences just as surely as the encouragement of growth has. At its best, sustained growth raises the poor out of poverty, improves the lives of the rich, and helps nations avoid intergenerational conflicts and the deprivations of fiscal crises. Even more basically, growth provides nations with the means and interest to protect the environment and to cultivate a vibrant and humane civilization.

We have highlighted the key role played by economic institutions in encouraging economic growth, taking Britain during and following the first Industrial Revolution as our first example. From it and from contemporary examples, we learn that governments can encourage sustained growth in part by establishing the rule of law, and securing and enforcing property rights, so that innovation is encouraged through economic incentives and the gains from technological change are widely dispersed.

With all that is at stake, it is sobering to see in history many examples of countries and eras in which growth flowered for a time but then evaporated.[64]

A vivid cautionary example of stunted economic growth, due in this case to institutional problems, is provided by China in the 1400s and 1500s. During that period, China's technology—exemplified in innovations such as the waterwheel and compass—was superior to Europe's. Yet Chinese technological change was not translated into sustained economic growth. Instead, having been established as a superior technology, its innovations hardened "into a custom immune to change."[65] The Chinese mandarinate as a centralized governing power resisted further changes that would upset the status quo and did not find it in their interest to pursue further innovations.

Here the Chinese experience contrasts with that of the United States, which originally decentralized political power through competition among rival states in a federal system. America enjoyed sustained economic growth during a second Industrial Revolution in the late 1800s, when innovations were pursued by competing centers of political power, which encouraged technological advances that brought commercial advantages.

Why does the United States not currently exhibit higher economic growth as a technologically advanced economy? If US technological change and research and development have been powerful forces in raising productivity and disseminating product innovations throughout much of our history, why in recent decades has economic growth in America slowed? The diminishing returns discussed in chapter 2 may be part of the answer, but other factors are also at work. The 1900s saw the United States increasingly concentrate civil authority at the federal level through a proliferation of regulatory agencies, with harmful consequences for the pace of technological innovation and sustained economic growth by the end of that century. For example, regulatory authorities have slowed the process of products reaching consumers, as when the Food and Drug Administration places severe constraints on the release of helpful new pharmaceuticals.

More broadly, American economic growth in recent decades has been imbalanced in being driven by consumption and debt. Rising debt has taken the form of increased consumer installment loans, larger credit card balances, and more home equity loans. The housing bubble of the early 2000s was also driven by leveraging, as households made smaller down payments and held larger mortgage loan balances in purchasing houses. Once the bubble burst, the US economy began to deleverage, that is, to save more and pay off debt. Recoveries from financial difficulties associated with leveraged financial bubbles are notoriously slow and anemic. America faces the challenge of achieving more balanced economic growth, characterized by higher levels of savings to fund increased investment in education, physical capital, and research and development.

To face these challenges well requires a clear sense of what is at stake in promoting, or not promoting, growth. The challenges will be best met when the US public understands the great value of growth, even for a society as wealthy as ours is. Continued growth, nudged toward the high end of the feasible range for

"Countries can embark on short-sighted policies and behaviors that produce temporary growth but end in pain and contraction. To get growth right takes wise choices and, at bottom, a citizenry willing to maintain and defend a culture that values human dignity, individual responsibility, trust, civic-mindedness, and other virtues. Economic growth can, in fact, help sustain these virtues and can encourage generosity and promote deeper relationships among peoples of differing racial, ethnic, and national identities."

cutting-edge economies, can confer tremendous gains in material well-being, including in such basic areas as life expectancy. It can equip us to care for the environment even more comprehensively and effectively than at present. It can smooth out harsh demographic and fiscal problems. Perhaps most significantly, it can simultaneously help the poor and better equip the rest of society to help them, two bright aspects of human flourishing.

To defend growth is not to say that every instance of growth is good or sustainable. Countries can embark on short-sighted policies and behaviors that produce temporary growth but end in pain and contraction. To get growth right takes wise choices and, at bottom, a citizenry willing to maintain and defend a culture that values human dignity, individual responsibility, trust, civic-mindedness, and other virtues. Economic growth can, in fact, help sustain these virtues and can encourage generosity and promote deeper relationships among peoples of differing racial, ethnic, and national identities.

The gains from growth are attainable anywhere. They know no boundaries of nation or location. Growth can deliver benefits for rich and poor societies alike. Rooted in the decisions of millions of persons and families and firms, growth's gains transcend those individual agents. Growth's promise endures.

RECOMMENDED
READING

Acemoglu, Daron, and James Robinson. *Why Nations Fail: The Origins of Power, Prosperity, and Poverty*. New York: Crown, 2012.

> Contends that human political and economic institutions, not culture or geography, are responsible for the wealth and poverty of nations. Examines the economic history of numerous regions and nations over the past 1,500 years in support of its thesis, contrasting cases of extractive and inclusive institutions.

Collier, Paul. *The Bottom Billion: Why the Poorest Countries Are Failing and What Can Be Done About It*. New York: Oxford University Press, 2007.

> Highlights the recent decline in global poverty while stressing the "traps" that stifle economic growth in fifty small developing economies and lock them into stagnant or declining living standards.

Easterly, William. *The Elusive Quest for Growth: Economists' Adventures and Misadventures in the Tropics*. Cambridge, MA: MIT Press, 2002.

> Describes in careful detail the problems arising when government agencies employ economic development strategies that ignore the role of incentives; discusses questions of debt forgiveness and corruption in connection to growth strategies for developing economies.

Fogel, Robert William. *The Escape from Hunger and Premature Death, 1700–2100: Europe, America, and the Third World*. Cambridge: Cambridge University Press, 2004.

> Provides in rich detail the story of how Europe and America have been freed from the chronic malnutrition

that was prevalent until roughly three hundred years ago. Describes the "technophysio evolution" process that has increased life expectancy and its connection to economic growth; also considers the health care challenges facing developing economies.

Friedman, Benjamin M. *The Moral Consequences of Economic Growth*. New York: Knopf, 2005.

Affirms and explores the role of economic growth in determining which countries bring political and economic freedoms to their citizenry. Discusses the history of thinking on economic growth and its moral benefits in Europe and the United States.

Helpman, Elhanan. *The Mystery of Economic Growth*. Cambridge, MA: Harvard University Press, 2004.

Seeks to unpack the sources of economic growth in terms of technological innovation, productivity, and economic and political institutions.

Lomborg, Bjorn. *The Skeptical Environmentalist: Measuring the Real State of the World*. Cambridge: Cambridge University Press, 2001.

Wide-ranging examination of data measuring human welfare, including empirical work on life expectancy, hunger, deforestation, energy, air and water pollution, biodiversity, and global warming; measures costs and benefits of economic growth and undermines popular beliefs about environmental degradation and overpopulation.

Mokyr, Joel. *The Enlightened Economy: An Economic History of Britain 1700–1850*. New Haven, CT: Yale University Press, 2009.

> Provides the story of Britain's explosive growth during the first Industrial Revolution, with an emphasis on changing demographics, changing attitudes toward entrepreneurship and commerce, and changing social norms.

Nallari. Raj, and Breda Griffith. *Understanding Growth and Poverty: Theory, Policy, and Empirics*. Washington, DC: World Bank, 2011.

> Sophisticated introduction to the extensive literature on the crucial role of economic growth in reducing poverty in the developing world. Discusses a wide range of policy challenges connected to disseminating the material benefits of economic growth.

North, Douglass. *Structure and Change in Economic History*. New York: Norton, 1981.

> Explains the major growth "revolutions" in Western economic history, including the European Industrial Revolution and its counterpart in America, using the tools of "new institutional analysis," i.e., property rights, incentives, transactions costs, and interest group dynamics.

Smith, Adam. *An Inquiry into the Nature and Causes of the Wealth of Nations*. 1776. Edited by R. H. Campbell and A. S. Skinner. Indianapolis, IN: Liberty Classics, 1981.

> The foundational work for classical political economy. Stresses the benefits of an extensive division of labor and

growing capital stock for economic growth as manifested in mid-eighteenth-century England and Europe. Packed with historical and empirical examples illustrating the factors that raise a nation's material living standards.

Van Til, Kent. *Less Than Two Dollars a Day: A Christian View of World Poverty and the Free Market*. Grand Rapids, MI: Eerdmans, 2007.
Critical examination of the features of free market economies, with an emphasis on distributional inequities; makes use of the theologian Abraham Kuyper and the political theorist Michael Walzer to present alternative economic arrangements aimed at providing distributional justice for the world's poor.

ENDNOTES

[1] Robert E. Lucas, "On the Mechanics of Economic Development," *Journal of Monetary Economics* 22 (1988), 5.

[2] Statistics here and in following paragraphs are from Angus Maddison, *The World Economy: A Millennial Perspective* (Paris: Organisation for Economic Co-operation and Development, 2001) unless otherwise noted; 1990 international dollars are adjusted by the authors for comparability to the US price level in 2012.

[3] World Bank, World Development Indicators, http://data.worldbank.org/data-catalog/world-development-indicators.

[4] Authors' calculation (in logs to account for nonlinearity) based on 2010 data from World Bank, World Development Indicators, http://data.worldbank.org/data-catalog/world-development-indicators.

[5] Robert William Fogel, *The Escape from Hunger and Premature Death, 1700–2100: Europe, America, and the Third World* (Cambridge: Cambridge University Press, 2004), 67-71.

[6] World Bank, World Development Indicators; data are 2009 purchasing power parity gross national income per capita.

[7] Adam Smith, *An Inquiry into the Nature and Causes of the Wealth of Nations* (1776), ed. R. H. Campbell and A. S. Skinner (Indianapolis, IN: Liberty Classics, 1981), 13.

[8] Ibid., 457.

[9] This is a consistently supported empirical finding in economics; trade and growth rise hand in hand. An introduction to the literature on this topic is Robert Baldwin, "Openness and Growth: What's the Empirical Relationship?" in *Challenges to Globalization: Analyzing the Economics*, ed. R. E. Baldwin and A. Winters (Chicago: University of Chicago Press/National Bureau of Economic Research, 2004), 499–521.

[10] Reported by the Bureau of Labor Statistics, based on data from the Current Population Survey for full-time wage and salary earners age 25 or older, at http://www.bls.gov/emp/ep_chart_001.htm.

[11] See Elhanan Helpman, *The Mystery of Economic Growth* (Cambridge, MA: Harvard University Press, 2004), 21–28.

[12] See N. Gregory Mankiw, *Macroeconomics* (New York: Worth, 2012).

[13] Nobel laureate Douglass North has been a leader in this effort. See, for example, Douglass North, *Institutions, Institutional Change and Economic Performance* (Cambridge: Cambridge University Press, 1990).

[14] Douglass North, *Structure and Change in Economic History* (New York: Norton, 1981); Douglass North and Barry R. Weingast, "Constitutions and Commitment: The Evolution of Institutions Governing Public Choice in Seventeenth-Century England," *Journal of Economic History* 49 (1989): 803–32.

[15] Daron Acemoglu and James A. Robinson, "Institutions as a Fundamental Cause of Long-Run Growth," in *Handbook of Economic Growth*, vol. IA, ed. P. Aghion and S. Durlauf (Amsterdam: North Holland, 2005), 389.

[16] Joel Mokyr, *The Enlightened Economy: An Economic History of Britain 1700–1850* (New Haven: Yale University Press, 2009), 368–69.

[17] Paul Collier, *The Bottom Billion: Why the Poorest Countries Are Failing and What Can Be Done About It* (New York: Oxford, 2007).

[18] David Dollar and Aart Kraay, "Growth Is Good for the Poor," *Journal of Economic Growth* 7 (2002): 195–225.

[19] US income earned by the lowest quintile fell from 4.4 percent (1975) to 3.4 percent (2007); see Jonathan Gruber, *Public Finance and Public Policy* (New York: Worth, 2011), 491.

[20] Richard Burkhauser, Jeff Larrimore, and Kosali Simon, "A Second Opinion on the Economic Health of the American Middle Class and Why It Matters in Gauging the Impact of Government Policy," *National Tax Journal* 65 (2012): 7–32.

[21] These and subsequent figures are taken from PovcalNet, the World Bank's online poverty analysis tool, http://iresearch. worldbank.org/PovcalNet/index.htm.

[22] Xavier Sala-i-Martin, "The World Distribution of Income" (NBER Working Paper No. 8933, Cambridge, MA, 2002).

[23] Paul Collier, *The Bottom Billion: Why the Poorest Countries Are Failing and What Can Be Done About It* (New York: Oxford, 2007). 11.

[24] See Branko Milanovic, *Worlds Apart: Measuring International and Global Inequality* (Princeton, NJ: Princeton University Press, 2005); and David Dollar and Aart Kraay, "Spreading the Wealth," *Foreign Affairs* 81, no. 1 (Jan./Feb. 2002): 120-133.

[25] World Bank, *World Development Report 2006* (Washington, DC, and New York: World Bank and Oxford University Press, 2006).

[26] See Paul Portnoy, "Environmental Problems and Policy: 2000–2050," *Journal of Economic Perspectives* 14 (2000): 199–206.

[27] See, for instance, Susmita Dasgupta, Benoit Laplante, Hua Wang, and David Wheeler, "Confronting the Environmental Kuznets Curve," *Journal of Economic Perspectives* 16 (2002): 147–68.

[28] See Wilfred Beckerman, *A Poverty of Reason: Sustainable Development* (Oakland, CA: Independent Institute, 2003) for a discussion of reserves of nonrenewables. Natural gas data are from US Energy Information Administration, www.eia.gov.

[29] Bill McKibben, *Maybe One: A Personal and Environmental Argument for Single-Child Families* (New York: Simon and Schuster, 1999), 77.

[30] For instance, the Copenhagen Consensus argues that it is wiser to address some of the consequences of global warming than to try to stop it entirely, because of the high value of other uses for the resources that would be needed to pursue the latter goal. See www.copenhagenconsensus.com/Projects/CCI2.aspx.

[31] William Cavanaugh, *Being Consumed: Economics and Christian Desire* (Grand Rapids, MI: Eerdmans, 2008), 91.

[32] Kent Van Til, *Less Than Two Dollars a Day: A Christian View of World Poverty and the Free Market* (Grand Rapids, MI: Eerdmans, 2007), 52–53.

[33] W. Douglas Meeks, *God the Economist: The Doctrine of God and Political Economy* (Minneapolis, MN: Augsburg Fortress, 1989), 161.

[34] Ibid., 57.

[35] Cavanaugh, *Being Consumed*, 91.

[36] Ibid., 93.

[37] Bob Goudzwaard, "Economic Growth: Is More Always Better?" in *Economic Justice in a Flat World: Christian Perspectives on Globalization*, ed. Steven Rundle (Colorado Springs, CO: Paternoster, 2009), 336.

[38] Ibid.

[39] Ibid., 340.

[40] Wendell Berry, *Home Economics: Fourteen Essays* (New York: North Point Press, 1987), and "The Idea of the Local Economy" *Harper's Magazine*, April 2002, 15-20.

[41] For instance, the Christian economist John E. Stapleford favors markets for promoting economic growth, yet expresses concern that preoccupation with a higher standard of living shrinks the amount of time people spend cultivating healthy family relationships. See *Bulls, Bears and Golden Calves: Applying Christian Ethics in Economics*, 2nd ed. (Downers Grove, IL: InterVarsity, 2009), 89.

[42] See, for instance, Jim Wallis, "When the Market Became God," chapter 2 in *Rediscovering Values: On Wall Street, Main Street, and Your Street—A Moral Compass for the New Economy* (New York: Simon & Schuster, 2010), 27-40.

[43] Rebecca M. Blank, "Viewing the Market Economy Through the Lens of Faith," in *Is the Market Moral? A Dialogue on Religion, Economics and Justice*, ed. Rebecca M. Blank and William McGurn (Washington, DC: Brookings, 2004), 38.

[44] Mokyr, *The Enlightened Economy*, 369.

[45] Ibid.

[46] Ibid., 372.

[47] Ibid., 373, 384.

[48] Francis Fukuyama, *Trust: The Social Virtues and the Creation of Prosperity* (New York: Free Press, 1995).

[49] Benjamin M. Friedman, *The Moral Consequences of Economic Growth* (New York: Knopf, 2005), 86-87.

[50] Ibid., 92.

[51] Blank, "Viewing the Market Economy," 38.

[52] Office of Management and Budget, *Economic and Budget Analysis*, February 2012, http://www.whitehouse.gov/sites/default/files/omb/budget/fy2012/assets/econ_analyses.pdf.

[53] Social Security Administration, "A Summary of the 2012 Annual Reports," http://www.ssa.gov/oact/trsum/index.html.

[54] Jonathan Gruber, *Public Finance and Public Policy* (New York: Worth, 2011), 107.

[55] Joseph Gagnon with Marc Hinterschweiger, *The Global Outlook for Government Debt over the Next 25 Years* (Washington, DC: Peterson Institute for International Economics, 2011).

[56] This is the debate about the size of the fiscal multiplier. Administration sources put its value at one or higher; critics such as Stanford's John Taylor put it around zero.

[57] Gruber, *Public Finance*, 117.

[58] The timing and consequences of fiscal crises are discussed in Carmen Reinhart and Kenneth Rogoff, *This Time Is Different* (Princeton, NJ: Princeton University Press, 2009); the US situation is discussed in Congressional Budget Office, "Federal Debt and the Risk of a Fiscal Crisis," *Economic and Budget Issue Brief*, Washington, DC, July 27, 2010.

[59] "Hyperinflation in Zimbabwe," Globalization and Monetary Policy Institute, Federal Reserve Bank of Dallas, February 2012.

[60] Raj Nallari and Breda Griffith, *Understanding Growth and Poverty: Theory, Policy, and Empirics* (Washington, DC: World Bank, 2011), 424.

[61] Barry Eichengreen, Donghyun Park, and Kwanho Shin, "When Fast Growing Countries Slow Down: International Evidence and Implications for China" (Cambridge, MA, NBER Working Paper 16919, 2011).

[62] Claude Menard and Mary Shirley, "Introduction," in *Handbook of New Institutional Economics*, ed. Claude Menard and Mary Shirley (Heidelberg: Springer, 2005), 4.

[63] Among many economic historians, see, for example, Daron Acemoglu and James A. Robinson, *Why Nations Fail: The Origins of Power, Prosperity, and Poverty* (New York: Crown, 2012), 89, on this point.

[64] Several examples are provided in E. L. Jones, *Growth Recurring: Economic Change in World History* (New York: Oxford, 1988).

[65] Nathan Rosenberg and L.E.Birdzell, Jr., *How the West Grew Rich: The Economic Transformation of the Industrial World* (New York: Basic Books, 1986), 137.

Edd S. Noell is chair of the Department of Economics at Westmont College. He has published (with Jim Halteman) *Reckoning with Markets: Moral Reflection in Economics* (Oxford UP, 2012) and serves as an associate editor of *Faith & Economics*. Noell's teaching and research interests center around the history of economic thought and financial markets.

Stephen L. S. Smith is professor of economics at Gordon College and a former visiting scholar at the US International Trade Commission. His teaching and research focus on international economics and economic development. Smith is coeditor of *Faith & Economics*, published by the Association of Christian Economists.

Bruce G. Webb is professor of economics, emeritus, at Gordon College where he taught macroeconomics for 35 years prior to his retirement in 2012. A financial market specialist, he is also a leading scholar of the morality of markets and economic systems. A founding member of the Association of Christian Economists, he served as coeditor of that association's journal, *Faith & Economics*, for 17 years.